MEREDITH® BOOKS DES MOINES, IOWA

Traditional Home® Easy Elegance
Editor: Linda Hallam
Contributing Editors: Diane Carroll, Catherine Hamrick,
Paula Marshall, Cynthia Pearson, Michael Rainey, Elle Roper
Art Director: The Design Office of Jerry J. Rank
Copy Chief: Terri Fredrickson
Copy and Production Editor: Victoria Forlini
Cover Photography: Gordon Beall
Editorial Operations Manager: Karen Schirm
Managers, Book Production: Pam Kvitne, Marjorie J. Schenkelberg, Rick von Holdt, Mark Weaver
Contributing Copy Editor: Jane Woychik
Contributing Proofreaders: Julie Cahalan, Becky Etchen, Heidi Johnson, Amy Panos
Indexer: Kathleen Poole
Editorial and Design Assistants: Kaye Chabot, Mary Lee Gavin, Karen McFadden

MEREDITH® BOOKS
Editor in Chief: Linda Raglan Cunningham
Design Director: Matt Strelecki
Executive Editor, Decorating and Home Design, Denise L. Caringer

Publisher: James D. Blume
Executive Director, Marketing: Jeffrey Myers
Executive Director, New Business Development: Todd M. Davis
Executive Director, Sales: Ken Zagor
Director, Operations: George A. Susral
Director, Production: Douglas M. Johnston
Business Director: Jim Leonard

Vice President and General Manager: Douglas J. Guendel

TRADITIONAL HOME® MAGAZINE
Editor in Chief: Ann Omvig Maine
Art Director: Kathryn Kunz Finney

MEREDITH PUBLISHING GROUP
President, Publishing Group: Stephen M. Lacy
Vice President-Publishing Director: Bob Mate

MEREDITH CORPORATION
Chairman and Chief Executive Officer: William T. Kerr

In Memoriam: E. T. Meredith III (1933-2003)

All of us at Meredith® Books are dedicated to providing you with information and ideas to enhance your home. We welcome your comments and suggestions. Write to us at: Meredith Books, Decorating and Home Design Editorial Department, 1716 Locust St., Des Moines, IA 50309-3023. If you would like to purchase any of our home decorating and design, cooking, crafts, gardening, or home improvement books, check wherever quality books are sold. Or visit us at: meredithbooks.com

Winston Churchill said, "We shape our buildings; thereafter they shape us." It's not such a leap to say the same of our rooms, the spaces where we spend our days and nights surrounded, if we're lucky, by the people and things that mean the most to us.

This book is designed to help you shape your rooms so they express *your* style by blending decorating styles. In *Traditional Home*₅ *Easy Elegance,* you'll learn how to liberate decorating with art and antiques from the period-room trap. Our homes are not museums. (Mine certainly isn't.) They are statements of who we are and what we like. As such, the old rules need not apply. This book exists to inspire you to mix and match periods, styles, and objects as you please, to live with your antiques and collections day to day instead of being afraid of them.

From French fauteuils and landscape paintings to Imari porcelain and tea caddies, the presence of objects that have special significance to their owners breathes life into a room like nothing else. But it's not just about the objects themselves, however beautiful or highly valued they might be. It's the way they are juxtaposed—the old with the new, the ornate with the simple.

Take, for example, a Southern plantation house where mahogany Federal furniture mingles with bold contemporary art against pristine gallery-like walls. Or, a little less extreme, a New York living room where a 1930s mirrored coffee table serves an 18th-century Italian fauteuil upholstered in red leather. These combinations work, often to stunning effect, because of the way the new throws the old into relief, and a richer experience of both is created.

Easy Elegance also offers a who's who of the big names in antique furniture, from William and Mary to the Louis styles to Chippendale and friends. Spotting fakes is a concern for many collectors, and we tell you how to use your eyes and hands to figure out whether what you have is the real thing or a clever reproduction. Of course, sometimes using a quality reproduction piece is the best choice, and you'll find advice for making the smart selections.

As well as adding layers of beauty and interest to a room, treasures collected from the past and given significance in today's living spaces make a statement that goes to the heart of the new traditional style: I respect the past, but I am not beholden to it. It's the only way to decorate—and live—that I know.

Ann Omvig Maine
Editor in Chief, Traditional Home

TABLE OF CONTENTS

BEAUTIFULROOMS

BEAUTY IN A ROOM IS HARD TO DEFINE, AND IS AS PERSONAL AND INDIVIDUAL AS IT IS IN A PERSON.

Yet for all the difficulty of categorizing beauty,

the quality of soul, of a depth and meaning beyond

the surface, stands out for both. The most beautiful

rooms are meaningful for their owners and guests.

No matter how rare and valuable the furnishings,

rooms are comfortable and inviting. They are rooms

for living, not the roped-off spaces of a museum.

Beyond the quality of the antiques and art, beautiful rooms are designed to create comfort for everyday living. Beautiful rooms also reflect the spirit of the inhabitants. For some lovers of modern art, that beauty lies in pristine, gallery-like settings where large abstracts pair with sleek mid-20th-century furniture. Collectors of 18th- and 19th-century furniture, traditional landscapes, and porcelain may find such spaces off-putting because many of them feel more at home surrounded by an abundance of treasures that is displayed in layers amid color and fabric.

Certainly significant art, collections, and furniture of antique (more than 100 years old) or notable provenance set the tone for beautiful rooms. But an assemblage of objects, no matter how fine, is only part of what makes a room beautiful. Collectors, interior designers, and architects who work with antiques and art address the intangibles—the soul and meaning of a room—as well as the tangibles of complementary backgrounds, lighting, editing, display, and supporting furnishings.

The soul of a room comes from people who inhabit it. Although it is possible to assemble exceptionally handsome rooms with the help of knowledgeable interior designers, antiques dealers, and art and lighting consultants, such rooms fall short if they are only stage sets for roles their owners want to play. A far more meaningful and beautiful room incorporates a person's history: a family piece, art purchased on a trip abroad, a painting selected out of passion rather than desired provenance. Such pieces are starting points for beautiful rooms, whether a person works with design professionals or designs his or her own spaces. The desire to have beautiful, personal rooms is an equally valid beginning. Rather than simply selecting antiques or art, thoughtful designers and art gallery owners can serve as teachers, helping interested clients focus on pieces that appeal and inspire.

Beyond a meaningful, special piece, the tangibles, starting with background and lighting, are the infrastructure of an elegant, polished room. No tangible is more important to art- or antiques-filled rooms than the backdrop of floors, walls, ceilings, and appropriate lighting.

When a room begins with significant art as the starting point, professional designers often take color cues from the major painting or paintings that will be displayed. White has been an accepted choice for the gallery-like displays often associated with contemporary art, but designers now sometimes recommend bolder colors such as yellow or red for dramatic backgrounds. When more traditional art will be displayed, designers may look for colors, such as sand, cream, or subtle tints, to set off the art and complement proposed fabrics and furniture without jarring contrasts. Ceilings may be tinted slightly paler than the wall color to avoid the starkness of white.

In traditional settings, deep vibrant hues (such as a rich red wallpaper or fabric walls) can be effective backdrops for art as well as porcelain. Patterned backgrounds of only two colors also work well: Striped wallpaper or toile fabric provide graphic punch without the visual confusion of multiple colors.

Lighting enhances art and furnishings—playing a supporting role, such as that of the ceiling-mounted directional-lighting often associated with contemporary art; or the more decorative picture lights, chandeliers, or sconces that illuminate traditional paintings. Table lamps also can anchor vignettes when arranged with small wall-mounted or tabletop artwork. As background and lighting are key elements of the ambience, furnishings are the glue that binds the disparate elements of a beautiful art- or antiques-filled room. When a special piece or two truly star in the room (a large abstract painting, a fine portrait, or a French armoire), other furnishings should be chosen to enhance the overall effect.

PAGE 8: A Regency console sets the tone for a stylish entry. PAGE 11: A collection of barley-twist candlesticks stands at attention on the stone mantel; the metal bird is a folk art piece. PAGE 13: Originally the living room of a weekend house, the library is now a grandly scaled venue for displaying art, antiques, books, and collections. Bookshelves rise to the ridge of the ceiling for maximum storage. The generous space allows the black-and-white art photograph to be the focal point for books, pottery, French olive oil pot, and lamp. A vintage hunting trophy adds a lodge ambience. Set off by the darkly stained oak floor, the table is Anglo-Indian, a highly prized style because of its relative rarity. The leather-upholstered armchairs are French Empire, left, and complementary American Empire, right. The exaggerated scale of American pieces, generally from the mid-19th century, distinguish them from the more delicately proportioned and detailed European pieces. A scattering of seashells contributes to the casual feel of the inviting room.

ABOVE: White walls, balanced by the rugless ebony-colored wood floor, set a gallery-like atmosphere in the polished living room. The well-edited furnishings range from the contemporary print framed in black to the traditional late-19th-century fauteuil-style armchair. The armless chairs work as transition pieces in the room of disparate elements. The geometric print introduces the lively yellow and pink tones that relax the tailored white sofa. OPPOSITE: A pair of Anglo-Indian cane-back chairs face the woven-rope coffee table, adapted from an African bed. Part of the collection of barley-twist candlesticks is displayed on English barley-twist side tables, and a Ross Bleckner sunflower print hangs above the sofa. The black lamps are chic accents against the crisp white walls.

DRAMA IN BLACK

Contemporary artwork pairs with a tantalizing amalgam of

American, European, Anglo-Indian, and African designs in a New

England weekend house full of colorful fabrics and exotic touches.

THE STYLIZED PAINTING RECALLS VAN GOGH'S FAMOUS 19TH-CENTURY SUNFLOWERS.

The graphic black-and-white palette organizes the living room, which has French doors opening to the garden. Newly upholstered in tufted black leather, the American Empire style sofa teams with French chairs and a pair of molded resin drum tables. The red and white toile introduces a scenic print, softening the hard edges of the art and lightening the heavy sofa. Slender contemporary picture lights illuminate the sleekly framed contemporary art. The English barley-twist candlesticks, part of a larger collection, and the small bronze sculpture on the gunmetal console table add traditional touches, while the yellow-and-pink paisley print is a modern twist on a classic fabric. The black lamp base and shade punctuate the scene and repeat the striking shade of the ebony floor. The overall effect is modern, livable, and utterly inviting.

Nineteenth-century art and antiques warm a New York City apartment dating from the architecturally rich Gilded Age. Shades of yellow and gold combine with edited art and accessories.

AGE OF INNOCENCE

An English linen press balances the trumeau-topped marble mantel in the grandly scaled living room. The fauteuil by the fireplace and the small gilded chair are French. The small piecrust accent table is English. The antique crystal chandelier and sconces balance the 14-foot-high ceiling. The early-20th-century Impressionist painting is *Spring Meadow in Lyme, Connecticut,* by Wilson Henry Irvine. Sunny yellow walls and simple silk drapery panels are in keeping with pared-down 21st-century styles.

CHINOISERIE PANELS

GRACE WALLS

OF A HEIGHT

THAT CALLS FOR

LARGE-SCALE

PRESENTATION.

Correctly scaled and beautifully detailed fine reproduction furniture and accessories, chosen to complement the proportions of the dining room, serve as the background for collected antiques. The pedestal table and reproduction Louis XVI-style flared-back chairs upholstered in two silk fabrics are stylish foils for the circa-1820 neoclassic dishes and tableware: crystal goblets, a bell-shaped decanter, and a rare amber cruet set. The antique French canvas chinoiserie panels are mounted above a classically styled credenza. The antique hurricane lights with brass bases and the birdcage fit the large scale of the room. Antique gilded sconces flank the fireplace. The footed porcelain vase is antique, while the candlestick is a new silver piece. In keeping with the neoclassical simplicity of the space, the silk drapery panels mimic the style in the adjoining living room; oversized silk tassels tie them back with casual sophistication. The vase on the mantel and the silver urn on the table filled with yellow echo the *Age of Innocence* ambience—a nod to the novel by Edith Wharton and its 1993 film adaptation. The airy yellow palette and tailored fabrics allow the furnishings to take center stage.

The cool colors the British used in

their steamy colonial outposts inspire

the ethereal blue palette for a living

room full of art, antiques, and vintage

furniture. Collected English boxes

add a personal touch to the look.

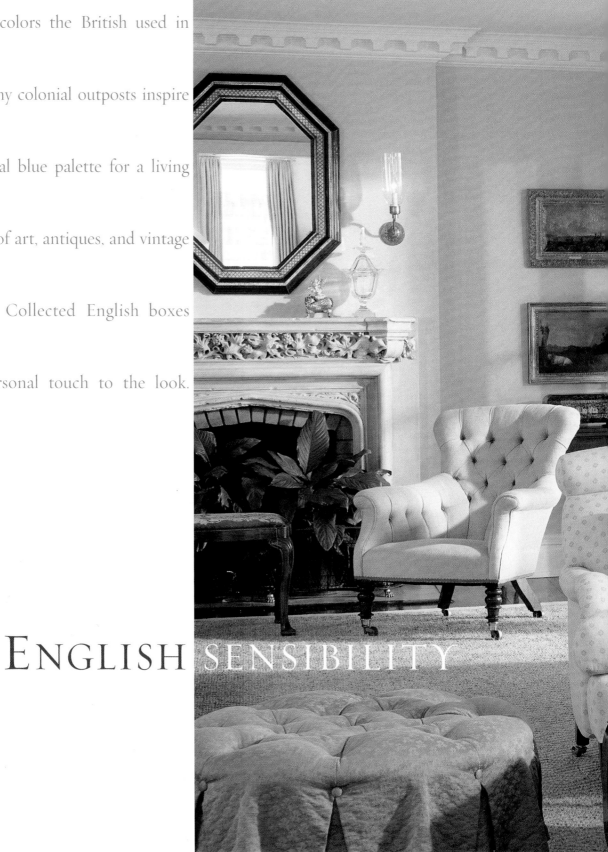

ENGLISH SENSIBILITY

Anchored by a period Oushak rug, this living room holds a mix of new and antique seating that creates a sense of modern comfort. Architectural detailing, such as the dentil molding added during a major remodeling, provides a suitable milieu for a handsome collection of British furniture and art. Famed English decorator Nancy Lancaster once owned the tufted "nursing chair" that now sits by the cast-stone fireplace. A caned William IV armchair, much prized by the Anglophile owners, is among the notable pieces. The steel engravings above the brass-and-glass table are by 19th-century English artist J.M.W. Turner. The oil landscapes also are 19th-century, as is the Irish crystal jar, one of a pair, on the mantel. Chosen for its octagonal shape, the mirror is a reproduction. Silk draperies are simple panels on brass rods. Crystal and glass accessories add interest without superfluous color.

Decorated in the same cool palette as the adjoining living room, the dining room is an ode to the enduring influence of British Colonial style. Fine reproductions mix freely with carefully selected antiques. A new crystal and silver-plated chandelier pairs with the 18th-century mercury glass sconce. The English-made reproduction double-pedestal table is a fine companion to the Scottish sideboard, circa 1840; both are mahogany. The painting, part of the owners' large collection of American and British landscapes, is 19th-century American in the style of the Hudson River School. The gilded frame and brass picture light are in keeping with the period of the painting. The rug is an antique Oushak, chosen for its subtle colorations and pattern.

OPPOSITE: A fine American bull's-eye mirror from the Federal period reflects the gracious dining room. The antique console table displays neatly arranged pairs of English mahogany knife boxes and quirky shell candleholders. A creamware tureen serves as a decorative container for a maidenhair fern. Reproduction dining chairs enjoy a tropical makeover courtesy of monogrammed linen slipcovers. ABOVE: Candle sconces, such as this 18th-century English etched mercury glass example, were popular in Sweden and other Northern European countries because they reflect and enhance the candlelight on long winter nights. Antique mercury glass, including American-made pieces, is a highly prized collectible that adds sparkle to traditional interiors.

RED REIGNS

A mirrored wall doubles the dramatic

impact of walls rich with color and

stacked with art. The large painting by

Esta Arkow is a stunning focal point.

A study in red, the living room of a New York apartment illustrates the power of color to highlight art and antiques. Paintings collected through the years include the A.H. Gorson to the left of the mirror and the Maurice Becker to the right. Two Tibetan monk figures face each other over boxes covered in quill, tortoiseshell, and ivory. The mirrored coffee table is 1930s Venetian, a period known for glamorous furniture. Equally chic is the late-18th-century Italian fauteuil, upholstered in dark red leather, to the left of the sofa. The repetition of red in the lampshades is the final touch on a stylish setting.

JUST THE RIGHT

SHADE OF RICH COLOR

CREATES A POWERFUL

BACKGROUND FOR ART,

SCENE-STEALING

ANTIQUES,

AND FLOWERS.

OPPOSITE: The mirror-framed mirror above the 19th-century chinoiserie commode reflects the focal-point painting. Based on Chinese decorative motifs and European interpretations of the exotic Far East, painted chinoiserie was especially popular in 18th- and early-19th-century French and English furniture. The stacked block prints and glass vase are more contemporary touches. An antique silver tray organizes crystal barware. RIGHT: Small framed watercolors are displayed on stands on a skirted round table. The tortoiseshell-motif glass bowl and the contemporary vase filled with yellow-and-red tulips complement without distracting from the focus on art. Frequently changing small paintings like these is a way to showcase pieces from a diverse collection.

Antique French fabrics combined with Italian

floral watercolors imbue a new villa-style house with

old-world ambience. The Oriental rug and antique

needlepoint are from the owners' collection.

FLORAL PRESENCE

Lovers of art and antiques may find their twin passions combined in rugs, needlepoint, and fabrics—collected textiles that add a richness and patina to rooms brimming with antiques. In this California living room, an antique valance and side panels frame the bay window, where woodwork is painted a trés appropriate French blue. Adding to the inviting scene and the mix of new and antique textiles is a collection of tapestry pillows on the window seat. New damask covers the small footstools that serve the reproduction upholstered armchairs. Flanking the windows are colorful painted roosters from Portugal perched on decorative brackets for a crowning finishing touch.

ABOVE: In a grand drawing room filled with treasures, antique Chinese vases on Georgian brackets flank the George III mirror. Chinese figures on the mantel also are antique. On the 20th-century shagreen coffee table, a copy of a custom design made for the Duchess of Windsor, sit twin obelisks that are antique French incense burners. The book-laden leopard-print ottoman stands on a goatskin rug, adding an exotic touch exotic to a room designed in the vein of a grand English country house. Highlighted by a gilded frame, the painting to the right of the mantel is a period piece. OPPOSITE: An Impressionist-style portrait by artist Henry R. Rittenberg anchors the wall above the sofa. Mirrored panels decorate the lacquered chinoiserie secretary. The smaller oil painting is deliberately hung at eye level for easy viewing from the chintz-covered armchairs.

Glazed and varnished plum walls, highlighted by pedigreed antiques

and fine art, set a lush scene. The opulent room is a perfect milieu for

the glittering 18th-century Russian chandelier.

AUBERGINEBEAUTY

A Georgian-style plantation house proves the perfect gallery for

Federal furniture and major paintings by 20th-century masters.

Diverse works find a common thread in artistic excellence.

FEDERAL MODERN

OPPOSITE: In the living room, *Heart* (1991) by Jim Dine hangs above a caned maple settee crafted in New England in 1820. From greatly different eras, bold design is the unifying element in this creative pairing. RIGHT: Two Andy Warhol Mozart lithographs (1986) group with a Donald Judd yellow, red, blue, and white wall sculpture (1986). American antiques include a pair of Pembroke tables (both 1800) flanking the Massachusetts-made Sheraton-style sofa (1810). The Sheraton armchair shown in the foreground is attributed to Ephraim Haines.

ABOVE: Without the distraction of rugs or window treatments, the library is a perfect showcase for the skill of late-18th- and early-19th-century American furnituremakers. A Hepplewhite console table (Charleston, 1810) takes center stage; the Hepplewhite sofa (1797) just beyond is attributed to Boston furnituremaker George Bright. The pair of unusual tub chairs, numbered 11 and 12, were originally made in 1797 as part of a set of 30 for the Massachusetts State House. One of the few English artifacts in the collection, the sailor was a trade sign for a ship's chandler; it has been authenticated to 1820. In the spare setting, the sailor is freestanding sculpture. OPPOSITE: Hung above a traditional mantel, one of the most recognizable pieces in the collection is the striking *Target* (1974), painted by Jasper Johns. The colorful upholstery of the Hepplewhite side chairs (Boston, 1805) as well as the graphic punch of the chairs' shieldback design create a visually pleasing arrangement with the painting. Restoration of the house, done to create gallery space for an extensive art collection, included the pale wood floors and the period mantel. However, moldings were deliberately left out of the turn-of-the-19th-century residence.

The open living room doubles as a gallery for late-20th-century art and American Federal-period furniture. French doors without window treatments flood the spacious room with natural light and offer views of the outdoors. Particularly striking is the *Love* sculpture (1990) by Robert Indiana. The sofa, detailed with "ears," was made by John Seymour in Boston in 1805. The lolling chair, upholstered in a bee print, was made by Joseph Short in Newburyport, Massachusetts, in 1810. The shieldback Hepplewhite chair (1810) is another Massachusetts piece, made in Salem. Occasional tables include a Hepplewhite Pembroke table (Baltimore, 1800), to the left of the sofa, and a marble-inlaid table, to the right of the sofa, made in Massachusetts in the early 19th century. Originally a London sofa table (1790), the coffee table features saber-style legs on casters that roll easily on the rugless, polished wood floor.

On the opposite end of the living room, *Dot* (1981) by Damion Hirst hangs above the circa-1800 Charleston-made mantel. A red, white, and blue *Star* (1972) by Robert Indiana hangs gallery-style—and leads the eye to the dining room beyond. *Black Poured Painting* (1995) by Ian Davenport, to the right of the fireplace, introduces a luminous surface. The two Sheraton Pembroke tables, made in either New York or Rhode Island in 1820, display glass pieces by Dale Chihuly. The bowl on the left was created in 1994, and the other was a commission in 1999. Other high-style American antiques in the room include a Federal worktable (1800) crafted in Boston by John Seymour and a Connecticut-made cherry candlestand table (1800) paired with the lolling chair. In this room, the mostly early-19th-century American furniture stands out as sculpture; in this pristine setting, the careful mix of tables and chairs ensures comfort.

OPPOSITE: In the entry, Susan Hutchinson's *Yellow* painting (1993) is an unexpected background for a Federal card table (New Hampshire, 1815) displaying George Rickey's stainless-steel *Spinners* sculpture (1988). The Sheraton side chair (1800) is a Philadelphia-made piece. ABOVE: In the formal dining room, Hepplewhite dining chairs (Baltimore, 1820) group with a new double-pedestal table crafted in Federal style. A New England mirror (1810) hangs above a Charleston sideboard (1810) displaying bronze figures (1990) by Lynn Chadwick. To the right of the doorway sits a Sheraton pier table with a sconce above, both crafted in Boston (1810). Here, as in all the home's major rooms, the collector-owners have carefully edited so the art and antiques are the focal point. The absence of a rug and the expected chandelier as visual anchors make the table and dining chairs appear to float on the bleached-wood floor. Unlike the other public spaces in the house, the dining room is devoid of major paintings. Instead, the traditional mirror above the sideboard serves as wall art. The doorway frames the view to the white stairwell and the large *Yellow* abstract by Susan Hutchinson.

Antique window cornices, cut down and restenciled for

a new location, neatly cap well-dressed windows in an

antiques-filled living room. A 1960s floor lamp adds a

touch of modern to update the handsome room.

CLASSIC CORNICES

Sunny yellow walls make a pretty backdrop for the dark wood tones of classic English antiques; the handsome 19th-century secretary stands out smartly, as does the fine French trumeau. Because the cornice and window treatments are the focal point, the new area rug is a neutral that adds texture without color. Lighthearted touches, such as the wall-hung painted clock and the reproduction Chinese garden stools serving as drink tables, relax the traditional mood. The reproduction upholstered pieces wear solids as well as an oversize checker design. The pretty floral draperies hint at sprightly English Country style.

YANKEE INGENUITY

Bright colors, cotton fabrics, and a touch

of the Paris flea market transform a mix

of collected New England furniture and

art into a lively decorating statement.

OPPOSITE: A casual mix of fabric remnants updates the fauteuil, left, and the wing chair. The rope sconces, newly topped with red shades, are from the Paris flea market. They flank a watercolor of New England seashells that leans on the mantel. Collected shells set the seaside summerhouse mood. Another nod to New England, antique quilts inspired the pattern for the hand-painted floor. BELOW: In this Nantucket weekend cottage, simple vintage pieces stylishly substitute for fine antiques. The coffee table, with a pleasing patina of age, started life as a plant stand. Interior designer Gary McBournie of Boston painted the traditional watercolors of shells specifically for the cottage. Boxes, baskets, and small pottery pieces are finds from antiquing forays in New England. The mix of seaside-cottage and country works well because the setting is a second home used primarily in the summer. The vintage furnishings add personality and warmth without the formality of more high-style pieces.

Traditional art such as these botanical prints of ferns, when framed and matted identically and hung in a grid pattern, takes on a contemporary look. Including the apple still-life varies the botanical theme for this garden house in a polished city setting.

BOTANICALLY INCLINED

In whites and naturals, the walls and sisal carpeting provide a subtle backdrop for the French chairs, updated in white upholstery fabric. The all-white scheme is the perfect counterpoint to dark antiques such as the English mahogany wall-hung corner cabinet. The cabinet also adds interest to a room that lacks architectural detail, successfully filling what could have been a dull corner of the apartment. The French coffee table, with a mirrored top, contributes a graceful shape to the space without overpowering the grouping. The fern prints, by various artists, were collected from old books over the years. Dramatic massing along with carefully spaced presentation produces more impact than had the prints been dispersed and hung on all the walls of the room.

OPPOSITE: An antique mirror reflects the collection of botanical prints in the living room. Architectural fragments add interest to the contemporary space. White upholstery on chairs with pale frames reinforces the ethereal quality of the neutral scheme. ABOVE: A colorful abstract painting, *Pre-pimientoed Olive Tree*, by Larry Benn, illustrates the visual energy of large-scale contemporary art in rooms of antique furniture—here the chest, trumeau, traditional collections, and accessories. The scale of the blue-and-white pottery jars gives the collection more presence than a similar grouping of small pieces. Fabric accents—from the zebra-print stool to the leopard-print pillow—finish the room in sleek, sophisticated style.

Exquisite French antiques, set off by luminous walls

and a new Aubusson rug, create a beautiful stage for

Italian and English accessories and contemporary art.

FRENCH FOUNDATION

An 18th-century Charleston house is the perfect setting for a cosmopolitan mix of antiques and art. In the living room, a painting in a traditional mat and frame by contemporary Charleston artist John Dunnan hangs above a 19th-century Adam-style mantel displaying Chinese export porcelain and metal flowers from an antique garden fence. Armless French chairs in the Louis XVI style complement the marble-topped table with an antique base. Pale green damask enhances the clean lines of the pair of new classic camelback sofas; pillows have been fabricated from antique textiles. An Italian cherub on a base, displayed on the bookcase to the right of the mantel, presides over the inviting room. The bookcases are filled with leatherbound books as well as English Staffordshire figurines and Chinese export porcelain.

RESTORATION
ADAM NICOLSON
COLEFAX & FOWLER
THE FRENCH INTERIOR
IN THE EIGHTEENTH CENTURY

OPPOSITE: Table lamps crafted from antique urns, the floor lamp, and the electrified crystal candle chandelier softly illuminate the grandly scaled living room. The French Regency-style coffee table adds handsome detailing with its tapered legs. BELOW: Framed to fit the space, the painting by California artist Arthur Beckwith introduces a dreamy landscape appropriate for the setting and scale. The bergère-style antique French armchairs covered in silk stripe face each other across the gilded coffee table—of unknown provenance, but a lucky flea-market find. The maple piano, an early-20th-century piece, recalls how formal parlors doubled as music rooms in 18th- and 19th-century America. A pair of small oil paintings, the top illuminated by a picture light for interest, stack in the corner behind the piano. The overscale tufted ottoman, upholstered in velvet and trimmed in fringe, is a nod to the comforts of late-19th-century rooms. The marble sculpture is a flea-market find. Although owned by antiques dealers who are avid collectors, the house is furnished with minimum accessories so that the antiques and art create comfortable but not cluttered rooms. In addition to the piece of European sculpture, a few selected Asian pieces, such as the horse on the coffee table, enliven the stylish mix.

ABOVE: In a master bedroom, an English fan cabinet and a Country French desk recall ladies' writing desks. Here the cabinet displays a collection of painted French and Chinese fans, indicative of 18th- and 19th-century Charleston. The armchair, updated with leopard-print fabric, is French. OPPOSITE: Two antique iron-and-crystal chandeliers balance the scale of the 17th-century French refectory table in the antiques-filled dining room. Lilies fill an antique wine cooler flanked by a pair of 19th- century French candelabra. Dining chairs upholstered in leather with nailhead trim are 19th-century French. A decorative candelabra and an ornate antique mantel clock group with the grandly scaled 18th-century tapestry above the mantel. Highlights from the owners' collection of Chinese rose medallion porcelain are displayed on the open shelves. Reflecting the scene is a 19th-century French mirror. The Italian bracket, one of a pair flanking the mirror, supports a footed urn that holds decorative metal flowers. The carved sideboard displays small bronze sculptures of classical figures, part of the owner's collection. Small landscape paintings in gilded frames, stacked for visual interest next to the door, are from the 19th century, a golden age for this art form.

Knowing the terms for antique styles and periods is just the beginning.

Understanding historical influences puts them into cultural context.

STYLE PRIMER

To fully appreciate furniture, collectors must study the whens and wheres of decorative arts history and the ever-changing tides of popular tastes. Collectors also need to keep in mind that antiques "of the period," rather than "in the style," means authenticity. In the United States during the 19th and early-20th centuries, tastes in European furniture generally paralleled settlement and immigration patterns. For example, collectors were more likely to find Dutch furniture in the Northeast, whereas French furniture was more common outside the major cities along the Gulf Coast. After World War II, population shifts and the growth of major cities in the Southeast and West spread these furniture styles across the country until regional tastes became more homogonized; some styles began to mirror trends in architecture and design.

At one time, French furniture defined Continental style. However, interior designers and collectors are increasingly interested in pieces from all European countries, with a noticeable surge in the popularity of Swedish furniture (strongly influenced at one point in history by the French). Collectors who favor classic English and American pieces may have noticed that standard terms such as Chippendale aren't always used. And with the 21st century still new, late-19th- and early-20th-century furniture, recently considered vintage, is now antique.

In some ways, the basic terms for French furniture are easier to understand than the terms for English pieces because of the accepted Louis styles numbered to correspond with the names of French monarchs, from Louis XIII to Louis XVI. However, complicating the timeline is popular French Régence, which is a transitional style between the rather heavy Louis XIV and the more feminine, curvy Louis XV. (Régence chairs, for example, can be identified by curved or cabriole legs.) The straight lines and classic architecture-influenced forms of Louis XVI style are a reaction to the curvy, decorative Louis XV forms. The popularity of Louis XV furniture inspired many imitations, still widely reproduced in Europe and America.

The French Revolution brought the Empire and Directoire styles; the Louis Philippe style, popular with collectors, emerged after the return of the monarchy.

French furniture styles influenced other European and American furnituremakers alike. Of particular appeal is the Swedish furniture crafted during the reign of King Gustav III, 1771-1792. This popularly sought style combines the elegant neoclassic lines and ornamentation of the Louis XVI style with boldness and whimsy. Swedish artisans toned down and mellowed the elaborate gilt surfaces of French furniture in order to display fine wood grain or subtle coats of muted pastel paint. According to history books, the Gustavian period ended in 1792, but the style remained popular until the mid-19th century. With their tapered legs and neoclassic motifs, high-style Gustavian pieces closely resemble Louis XVI, but the shapes are bolder and have fewer sharp angles and less ornament, such as the ormolu detailing favored in France. Like the Louis styles, Gustavian also enjoyed a revival from 1900 to the mid-1940s, which was the advent of the midcentury Swedish styles.

The highest styles of Swedish furniture from the true Gustavian period are difficult to locate. Such pieces were not imported in great quantity in the 19th and 20th centuries, when

19TH-CENTURY LOUIS XVI

18TH-CENTURY LOUIS XVI

19TH-CENTURY LOUIS XVI

19TH-CENTURY FRENCH RÉGENCE STYLE

19TH-CENTURY FRENCH RÉGENCE STYLE

19TH-CENTURY FRENCH

18TH-CENTURY SWEDISH

19TH-CENTURY SWEDISH

19TH-CENTURY DUTCH

19TH-CENTURY CONTINENTAL

18TH-CENTURY ENGLISH LATE CHIPPENDALE

EARLY-19TH-CENTURY ENGLISH HEPPLEWHITE

18TH-CENTURY ENGLISH GEORGE III

19TH-CENTURY ENGLISH REGENCY

18TH-CENTURY AMERICAN QUEEN ANNE

18TH-CENTURY AMERICAN WINDSOR

20TH-CENTURY BRIGHTON PAVILION REPRODUCTION

19TH-CENTURY CHINESE

French and English styles were de rigueur among tastemakers, and authentic pieces are no longer allowed to leave Sweden.

Fortunately for collectors who want period pieces from overseas, English antiques continue to be imported. The style and period terms used in the United States can be confusing, especially because of the influence of English craftspeople on American Colonial style. During the late 17th and early 18th centuries, colonial American furnituremakers followed the English pattern of classifying the style by the name of the English monarch reigning when the style was introduced, rather than by the designer's name or a descriptive name. This practice ends with the Georgian period when American furnituremakers diverged from the English naming system.

Collectors of English antiques require a short course in English history starting with George I, who followed Queen Anne and was followed by George II and George III. George IV is commonly called English Regency (named for the years when the future George IV was regent, not yet king,). This furniture resembles the neo-classical French Directoire and Empire styles that were strongly influenced by Greek, Roman, and Egyptian motifs.

What Americans often think of as the classic Chippendale chair dates stylistically to the early Georgian era. And what is now called Hepplewhite dates to the George III period. Because of the American Revolution and the colonists' animosity toward the king of England, the furniture terms of George I, II, and III never caught on in the United States. (Americans, however, have not been as averse to using the terms William IV, Victorian, and Edwardian for the periods that followed.) Instead, Americans gravitated to the term Chippendale for the furniture influenced by the designs of Englishman Thomas Chippendale, who published a famous furniture design book in 1754. Chippendale's designs took already fashionable shapes and applied rococo swirls, shells, and flowers, along with chinoiserie fretwork, pagoda crests, and the quatrefoil shapes of Gothic taste. Chippendale popularized the ribbon-back chair; the design has, with variations, remained a staple in Europe and America.

While Chippendale was a major tastemaker in the British Isles, his books were the single greatest influence on American furniture in the late 18th century. In the colonies, wealthy patrons in the seaports of Philadelphia, Newport (Rhode Island), Charleston, Boston, and New York had cabinetmakers copy pieces from Chippendale's patterns. Although furniture made in each city had slight variations, most American Chippendale pieces are simpler and more conservative than the English-made pieces. American furnituremakers favored highly patterned Santo Domingo mahogany for detailing. Rococo-style ornament was more popular than Gothic or chinoiserie, and the ball-and-claw foot of the earlier Queen Anne style, no longer fashionable in England, was popular in the colonies and the young United States. The term Chippendale was not, however, widely used until the American Centennial of 1876 sparked the craze for Colonial Revival furniture.

Another 18th-century furniture designer, George Hepplewhite, also greatly influenced European and American styles. His much-emulated designs featured heart- and shield-shape chair backs detailed with carved motifs of wheat, ferns, swags, and feathers. His work is identified by delicately grooved and fluted chair legs and spade-shape feet.

Also influential has been the work of anonymous English furnituremakers who designed the first Windsor chairs in the early 18th century. While Chippendale introduced a pierced splat between the rods of the back, craftspeople in colonial America created the many variations that remain popular. The chairs are often categorized by the type of back they have, such as loopback or fanback.

At the close of the 19th century, the Art Nouveau movement introduced pieces with sinuous lines and ornamentation in France, and Charles Rennie Mackintosh popularized pieces with severe lines in Scotland. In the 20th century, the sinewy lines of Art Deco gave way to the glamour of Art Moderne in furniture of the 1930s and 1940s. Throughout the 20th century, however, the popularity of reproductions here and abroad proved that the good designs from earlier centuries is timeless.

COLLECTING

ASK ANY COLLECTOR WHY SHE OR HE COLLECTS AND WHY SHE OR HE CAN'T SEEM TO STOP.

One day an Imari porcelain bowl, a small oil seascape, or a miniature chair passed over for years in an antiques store suddenly catches the eye. One purchase leads to another and another. A collection is born. Something about the object—its color, shape, history—has an appeal that sets off an association or memory for the collector. As with any addiction, one is never enough.

For some collectors, the search and acquisition are as important as, if not more than, ownership. Others inherit a collection that was lovingly assembled and passed down through the generations; for them, the passion of the past is part of the present.

While it is possible to reap financial returns on collections, antiques dealers, art dealers, and appraisers caution that it takes expert knowledge, timing, and, most likely, rather sizable initial investments. Very fine or rare antiques, such as 18th- or 19th-century English or French furniture, or comparable American furniture made by English-trained craftspeople, appreciated in value far more than mass-produced Chippendale-style furniture made for the American Centennial in the 1870s. Dealers advise collectors to purchase high-quality pieces that they like and will enjoy, even without the expectation of major financial gain, rather than thinking of collecting in financial terms. Because of the vast size of the United States and the multitude of cultural influences within its borders, some collectors favor simple regional styles such as the plain furniture crafted in 19th-century workshops in New England or pieces made by German craftspeople in the Hill Country of Texas.

To create collections that contribute to a beautiful, well-designed home requires thought, knowledge, discipline, and patience. The best advice from dealers and appraisers is the simplest: Take it slow. Novice collectors who yearn to acquire majolica porcelains or 19th-century engravings of Roman ruins, for example, are advised to read books and magazine articles and to look and ask questions before they buy. (Potentially serious collectors may want to attend seminars or take antiques courses offered as adult education by some colleges and communities.) Museums, galleries, art shows, and antiques shops and shows are ideal venues for seeing antiques and art and, in the case of shops and shows, examining objects up close. Reputable dealers answer questions, explaining signs of quality or areas that are subject to fakery. Dealers also help collectors locate pieces and trade up, a useful service as one becomes more serious about a collection.

True collectors, who love the act of collecting, often have several collections in different phases. Perhaps the collector has been assembling Imari porcelain, landscape paintings in the Hudson River School style, and English Regency furniture for years. The three collections, along with some judiciously selected antique Oushak rugs, comfortably furnish the living room. Meanwhile, in the dining room, the beginnings of a new interest in Old Paris porcelains mingle with an earlier passion for 19th-century Tiffany silver. In the master bedroom, an antique botanical print received as a gift has led to some careful inquiries at shops that deal in 17th- and 18th-century Dutch tulip prints and to a new wall color to better show them off. In the breakfast room, a collection of transferware plates is often part of everyday meals and casual entertaining.

The joy of collecting over time is that the collections are integrated into the design scheme of the home and into daily life. Collections are lived with, enjoyed, and used as a matter of course— perhaps with the thought that they one day may be enjoyed by the next generation. Or, there may come a time when a collection no longer works. When someone moves to a different residence or another part of the country, the perfect collection may no longer seem to fit. Then it may be time to sell or give away the collection, keeping only a few special pieces that meld with the new décor. For a true collector, such a bittersweet parting offers some solace: the opportunity to start from scratch, assembling a fresh collection that fits well into another chapter of life's design adventures.

PAGE 62: Six lithographs by French artist Henri Matisse hang grid-style above a mid-20th-century cabinet crafted in France in the style of influential postwar furniture designer André Arbus. The lithographs are from a larger collection assembled by a French doctor and later purchased by an American interior designer. PAGE 65: European glassware, including the yellow stoppered bottle, adds punches of color in a room that showcases the pale wood furniture associated with mid-20th-century French design. PAGE 67: In the entry of a city apartment, 18th-century Italian chairs with seats newly recovered in robin's-egg blue leather flank a finely detailed copy of a mirrored French commode from the mid-20th century. Because of a low ceiling, a new custom mirror, purposefully smaller than comparably styled vintage mirrors, neatly fits the space. The lamp is Venetian, with a faceted glass finial and custom-designed square shade. The opaline-and-gold glass pieces on the commode are from mid-20th-century Italian glassmaker Barovier and Toso. The mix of the French- and Italian-style pieces reflects a 21st-century design trend—combining Continental styles.

FRENCHMIDCENTURY

Before and after World War II, French artisans designed

sleek furniture now popularized by 21st-century trend-

setters drawn to its simple shapes and luxury materials.

Midcentury French furniture—from the pair of armchairs and pigskin-upholstered bench to the Mario Quarti coffee table—anchors the living room of a high-rise apartment. The sofa is a French 1940s-style reproduction. Six Matisse lithographs, part of a collection originally assembled by a French doctor, hang above a cabinet in the style of French postwar furniture designer André Arbus. In addition to sleek curved lines, hallmarks of midcentury French furniture include mirrored surfaces and burled and inlay detailing like the sun-spray design on the console (see page 62). Light and transparent, glass lamps are apropos for the glamour of the room.

OPPOSITE: The cabinet, inspired by the work of French furniture designer André Arbus, incorporates a sun-spray design and bronze fittings. Designers such as Arbus based their unadorned designs on the more ornate French furniture forms from the Directoire and Louis XVI periods. Compared to 18th- and 19th-century designs, 20th-century furniture designers crafted larger pieces, often with chunkier legs, and replaced elaborate carvings and opulent detailing such as ormolu with curved shapes. The X form in postwar furniture is associated with Arbus and designers inspired by his work. ABOVE: Here a 19th-century Romantic painting in a traditional frame hangs above an early-1930s French Art Deco burled walnut cabinet with glass shelves. American Art Deco furniture has a more streamlined look, whereas French pieces of the same period tend to be more decorative, as the marble top and fittings of this piece suggest. The striped lamp, a 1950s Murano glass by Dino Martens, is an equally glamorous piece.

BELOW: Originally used in city residences to make rooms look larger and to reflect objets d'art, mirrored screens recall the glamour of mid-20th-century design. The 1930s French screen in this dining room features mirror-on-mirror detailing. OPPOSITE: Oversize pieces, such as this 1940s French mirror in a formal dining room, showcase the exuberant design of the era. Instead of the elaborate frames of 18th- and 19th-century mirrors, examples from the pre- and postwar period often incorporate mirror on-mirror detailing. The diamond and star motifs are likewise hallmarks of the era. Earlier Art Deco pieces, particularly those in pale finishes, work well with the sleek midcentury design, as evidenced by the successful pairing of the 1920s dining chairs, based on the Greek klismos form, with the glass-top pedestal table. The chandelier is a midcentury Venetian design. Small paintings purchased in France and a plaster artist's model round out the setting.

OPPOSITE: In keeping with the luxurious bedrooms associated with the 1940s, pale champagne walls complement the delicate 19th-century Venetian mirror and the padded and shirred-silk headboard, a new custom piece inspired by upholstered beds of the period. The night table is a mirrored 1930s French commode; the lamp base is alabaster. A nude etching, matted and framed, adds interest without the distraction of unnecessary color. At the end of the bed, a stool with an X-shaped base emulates the style of André Arbus. ABOVE: A richly detailed, mirrored dressing table recalls the sophisticated, worldly style of mid-20th-century design popularized in films of the era. The dressing table is a fine example from the well-known French Jansen line, highly prized by collectors of midcentury French furniture. The table is noteworthy for its stylized etched and chiseled gold-and-clear-glass apron. The Florentine mirror hung above, with a beautifully detailed frame, reflects the Venetian mirror hung on the opposite wall. The tufted slipper chair with shirred cushion and stylized saber leg illustrates the luxe style of the period.

Blue walls—inspired by a Chinese exportware plate—create

a dramatic canvas for English antiques and period treasures.

BRITISHBLUE

OPPOSITE: The wide range of periods and styles represented in this room is indicative of grand English houses and the ever-popular design direction they have inspired: An English Regency table grouped with cane-back armchairs serves as the coffee table; the Pembroke table, with its signature drawer set in the apron and pedestal base, divides a pair of fauteuil-style, carved armchairs. Chinese exportware fish plates are displayed with the sculpture on the table. Illuminated by a picture light, the grandly scaled oil painting hangs above a gilded console table, with its vignette of clock and candelabra. ABOVE: The antique linen press, the owner's first serious antique, charted blue design direction for this city condominium decorated in English Country House style. The grand scale of the space helps create the drawing-room ambience, enhanced by the mix of armchairs, side tables, and classic botanical prints. Above the fireplace, a grand English mirror flanked by sconces reflects the handsome room.

World-traveling collectors settle their treasures into a

Federal-style house, creating a comfortable 21st-century space.

REFINEDMIXING

The owners of this 19th-century Federal-style house chose pieces according to personality, not period or provenance—although French does seem to be the favorite. Included in this stylish amalgamation are a French farm table and an Italian garden bench. Also French are the gilded, armless Louis XVI-style chairs, pulled from the wall when extra seating is needed. French city and country pieces mix well with the Parisian wire chandelier and the rustic antique chest from Normandy, topped by a reverse-painted French mirror. (The tray in front is painted tole.) The chinoiserie secretary, used to store china and crystal, and the unusual Italian enamelware wall sconce with leaf motif contribute to the international feel. Rather than a predictable urn or bowl, a spherical topiary form serves as a striking see-through centerpiece. What makes the mix work: a clean, neutral backdrop, the absence of window treatments, minimal fabrics, and pared-down but scaled-up accessories.

Classics in their own right, French pieces from the 1930s through the 1950s imbue a room

with fashion-forward, furniture-as-art good looks and a plethora of sophisticated comforts.

FRANÇAISMODERN

Furniture in the style of famous mid-20th-century French furniture designers makes up a retreat where relaxation is as important as world-class design. Anchoring the generously proportioned room is a parchment-and-oak console table by Jean Michel Frank, a well-known and influential midcentury French furniture designer. Goblet-style lamps feature wooden bases. The wrought-iron-framed mirror is suspended from ceiling molding by a heavy decorative rope. The rug, an Art Deco design from the 1920s, contributes stylized pattern typical of the era. Other furnishings of note include the oversize leather-and-metal coffee table and the leather-and-metal armchair to the left, designed in the style of Jean Michel Frank by Giacometti. The camelback sofa, just visible in the bottom left corner, and the leather club chair with rolled back also are based on Frank designs and illustrate his long-lasting influences on sleek, modern furniture styles. The leather-and-wood tray table is an early-20th-century piece. An array of accent pieces—from the Thebes stool to the Asian root bowl on the coffee table, to the trio of metal sculptures on stands—add to the multicultural mix.

ABOVE: The dramatic art piece hung above the Beaux Arts mantel is *Broken Eugena* (1996–97) by Graham Gilmore. The pair of 1940s French chairs flanking the fireplace recall the influence of African art on 20th-century designers and artists. A particularly striking and rare piece is the oak-and-lion's-skin armchair to the right of the fireplace. Bookshelves display an array of objects from around the world—including pewter vases and bowls, a pink glass vase, a Swedish ball on stand, an African headrest, an English pottery bowl, a wooden Shaker box, and an Art Deco watercolor. Adding sculptural shapes against the white background are French tole containers and a black chinoiserie vase. Art books recall the continuing influence of 20th-century modern masters, such as Picasso. OPPOSITE: The side or hall chair is a French walnut piece from the 1940s, a stylized version of 19th-century hall chairs. Design books reiterate the influence of Alberto Giacometti and Jean Michel Frank on 20th-century design.

In a clean, white setting, traditional landscape paintings bring the serene beauty

of 19th-century style to the sophisticated living room of a 21st-century collector.

LANDSCAPELOVER

ABOVE: Collectors fill their homes with their passions, as the living room and adjoining sunroom of this city condominium attest. The interest and the beauty of the collection lies in its unity—nearly all are 19th-century pastoral landscapes inspired by the Hudson River School and other regional styles; some seascapes are also included. For the young collector, a flea market devotee, the style and beauty of unrestored paintings and their sometimes worn frames are more interesting and appealing than their provenance. The easel offers a convenient way to rotate paintings in an expanding collection; the windowsill in the sunroom serves the same purpose. OPPOSITE: Two landscape paintings in classic gilded frames stack above the 19th-century American mahogany chest. A prayer chair, one of a pair found at a farm sale, holds antique books that can be cleared away when extra seating is needed. The tole coffee table is a French antique. An antique American quilt, chosen to complement the green and camel colors in the landscape paintings, adds texture to the white slipcovered sofa.

LEFT: Windowsills and a radiator cover offer display space in the sunroom. (Paintings and accessories are moved away from the heat when the radiator is in use.) The ball-and-claw-footed game table and two pairs of chairs are 19th-century antiques. Flirty slipcovers update the traditional chairs. The pale background and window shades allow the paintings to star; the leopard print interjects a lively touch that relaxes a room of traditional art and antiques. ABOVE: Landscape paintings hang on every available wall—including above an antique Biedermeier side chair—to molding height. The stacked arrangements help to organize the smaller paintings in the collection. The Biedermeier chair, associated with early-19th-century German furniture styles in the neoclassic mode, may have also been made in Austria, where the strong, clean lines of the design also enjoyed popularity.

Fine American antiques set the stage for an equally noteworthy collection

of antique English tea caddies and a striking contemporary painting.

AMERICANBEAUTY

ABOVE: In a collector's home, antique Irish mirrors with the patina of age hang above a fine sideboard (circa 1910). The Biedermeier tea caddy is part of an extensive collection; such beautifully crafted pieces illustrate the importance of tea in the 18th and 19th centuries. Chinese porcelain plates on stands flank the tea caddy. OPPOSITE: Contemporary art brings modern sensibilities to rooms, such as this dining room furnished with fine period antiques and collections. The dining table and the side chairs are 19th-century American. Two pairs of silver candlesticks, from Ireland circa 1790, group with a porcelain bowl placed on a rosewood stand.

A FINE CHEST-ON-CHEST.

ABOVE: A living room admirably serves as a decorative arts gallery for a collection of delicate Chinese export porcelain. The symmetrical pairing of objects on the shelves—for example, the roosters and the bowls—helps to visually organize an array of shapes and sizes. By not crowding the shelves, the collector allows the porcelain to stand out as objects worthy of interest. The addition of the built-ins created safe display, and also created a niche to display an 18th-century American chest. The American Queen Anne chair is circa 1760. OPPOSITE: The collector's library offers additional display area with a built-in that organizes porcelains as well as antique tea caddies and leatherbound books. The spare, symmetrical arrangement and the use of pairs of objects gives order and logic to what could be an overwhelming collection of beautiful objects and museum-quality books. The English chest-on-chest has elevated block feet typical of the period and is noteworthy for the concave inlay at its base. The table to the left is an English architect's table from the turn of the 19th century; the table with drawers (in the foreground) is Irish, circa 1760, indicative of the furnishings crafted for manor houses.

ABOVE: A collector of American and English antiques chooses a pared-down approach—and a symmetrical arrangement—to show off his treasures. An 18th-century English mirror with its original glass hangs above wainscoting surrounded by Italian architectural drawings. The dropleaf Kentucky table displays English Sheffield candlesticks, a silver vase, and an ivory casket (box). OPPOSITE: Display is everything in a library devoted to collections. Of particular interest are the prized 18th-and 19th-century miniatures, including the two smaller-scale secretaries (both from Pennsylvania) on the left, a Virginia-made chest, and a New York chest, right. The full-size chest displays a miniature secretary, circa 1800, traced to either New England or Pennsylvania. The pair of Windsor chairs are examples of American craftsmanship. The chair to the left is New England, circa 1790; the chair to the right is New York, circa 1830.

Before the Industrial Age, furnituremakers concentrated on what

was visible to the eye, leaving interior parts of a piece unfinished.

REAL/FAKE?

The antiques collector who claims to have never been fooled simply hasn't realized it yet. Because recognized antiques are valued far beyond their original function, furniture has been altered—and at times outright faked—since the concept of "antique" began.

Most collectors, whatever their degree of knowledge and experience, make an occasional mistake. But a wealth of scholarly and popular books and magazines provide information on lines, proportions, wood, carving, and other detailing—all to help novices and experienced collectors avoid making unwise purchases.

To buy authentic antique pieces, a collector needs to become familiar with terms and characteristics of styles and schools. Points to consider: Is a style generally curvy, or are most of the lines straight and the shape boxy? Does the style appear delicate or hefty, or something in between? How do details and choice of wood contribute to the general appearance?

In furniture making, patterns and design change over time and distance, resulting in different styles and regional variations. Old reproductions often mix styles; fakes and frauds may mix regional characteristics. To help people recognize style and regional variations, experienced collectors and dealers stress the

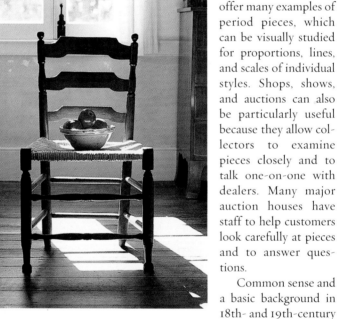

importance of seeing as many objects as possible by visiting museums, historic houses, and antiques shops, auctions, and shows.

Although museums won't allow students to touch furniture, they offer many examples of period pieces, which can be visually studied for proportions, lines, and scales of individual styles. Shops, shows, and auctions can also be particularly useful because they allow collectors to examine pieces closely and to talk one-on-one with dealers. Many major auction houses have staff to help customers look carefully at pieces and to answer questions.

Common sense and a basic background in 18th- and 19th-century history are also valuable tools in authenticating furniture. In this period of fine craftsmanship, furnituremakers had abundant supplies of superb wood but limited time to create their pieces. Because excellent timber supplies allowed for selectivity well into the 19th century, only high-quality materials were used. While period cabinetmakers with access to fine wood avoided wood with knots or wormholes, later restorers and fakers were much more likely to use inferior wood.

Colonial cabinetmakers also preferred wide boards, partly because the supply was plentiful and also because it was easier and faster to work one board than to put several boards together to form a surface. Occasionally cabinetmakers used two boards for a tabletop or case top, but they preferred using a single wide board. Three or more boards on a table or chest top suggest a suspect lineage.

While period furnituremakers had plenty of fine woods, time was precious because all work had to be accomplished entirely by hand during daylight hours. Furnituremakers, by necessity frugal with their labors, did not paint or stain any wood that did not show. For example, staining the undersides of chests or tables was a waste of labor, time, and materials.

The back of the chest, the bottom of the drawer, or the inside of a seat rail— all areas generally not seen—were left rough with the signs of the woodworker's tools still visible. If such structural elements have been finished (i.e., sanded smooth, shellacked, or varnished), they are not original.

In contrast, the outright faker or legitimate repairer could afford to spend the extra time and effort. Evidence of careful finish work on hidden surfaces identifies postperiod work. Legitimate repairs and alterations of a piece is to be expected but, depending on the extent, lessen an antique piece's value.

Hidden repairs or alterations can be hard to detect, but visible wood is an excellent medium for the investigator who wants to judge the age of an antique. This is because wood shrinks naturally with age. It also holds tool marks, and it scars, wears away with use, and changes color with time. All of these characteristics provide clues to the potential buyer who takes the time to carefully look and consider the effects of age and natural wear.

As wood dries out, it shrinks into the grain. This process goes on for years as the fibers expand and contract with the seasons, in direct correlation to the moisture in the air. One of the most obvious places to look is on any surface that started life as perfectly round. This could be a tabletop or a spindle of a chair. With the passage of time, such pieces eventually become "out of round."

This means the diameter of a 200-year-old tea table with a round top could be as much as three-quarters of an inch different when measured in two different points. Age shrinkage becomes more apparent in many less obvious ways as well. Panels constrict across the grain. Over a period of time these panels often shrink enough to create a visible gap between the panel and the framing.

In other forms of case furniture, the effects of shrinkage are observed in drawers. Drawer bottoms are almost always of one piece of wood. Because the sides of the drawer are relatively thin, the grooves that the bottom board rests in are comparatively shallow.

As wood shrinks, the drawer bottom pulls out of the grooves, creating a gap. Another effect of shrinkage in case pieces with drawers is that the sides of the case itself will shrink, causing drawer fronts to protrude slightly.

Joinery, too, can provide clues about furniture aging. Any time one piece of wood is joined to another at a right angle, a slight misalignment of the joint or a crack will appear over time and is to be expected. As wood shrinks with time, flat surfaces, such as tabletops and the sides of chests, develop an uneven or wavy surface. A perfectly smooth surface indicates new wood added or a harsh refinishing process.

Refinishing drastically lowers value, so patina is a crucial element to look for in antique furniture. Patina is an accumulation of dirt, wax, and soot, which combines with the oxidation of the surface that, over the years, ages and mellows the piece. Patina gives the rich surface that only the passage of time can accomplish. Frequently it is apparent from the outer surface of a piece whether it possesses an old original surface or has been refinished.

Patina work is an analytical tool in studying the interior and bottom of a piece, but it is indispensable when analyzing exterior surfaces. A recognized method of distinguishing stain from oxidation is to scratch the surface with a fingernail. If the surface has darkened with time, the oxidation is only on the surface, so the scratch will expose raw wood. If the piece has been artificially aged, the stain is absorbed into the pores of the wood. The scratch will remain basically the same color.

To get a complete view, it's equally important to study the entire piece. The underside or interior surfaces of a piece of furniture provide the visible clues to age, such as old tool marks or a history of fasteners such as screws and nails. It is also here that patina develops over glue blocks, runners, and secondary woods. The replacement of a top, the loss of glue blocks, or any repairs to the case become evident when different colors emerge, disturbing the continuity of the interior patina.

The woods themselves provide many of the clues. New wood is surprisingly light in color. Darkened secondary woods are hallmarks of time and can be easily read if a buyer takes the time and care. A point of reference is wood's natural discoloration and wear over the years.

When wood darkens naturally, it does so only on the surface; the wood beneath remains protected from the air. Newly exposed wood—freshly sawn, cut, or abraded—is light, almost bright. Unless stained or artificially aged, it stands out.

Fakers and restorers sometimes use old wood in repairs or embellishments, but it must be cut to fit, leaving small surfaces of new wood exposed. To mask the fresh-cut wood, most defrauders turn to stain, sometimes coffee or tea. Any staining of an unfinished surface is a sign of trouble. Such work was not economical, and period craftspeople were economical, not wasting their time or materials to finish secondary surfaces.

Creating a good fake is a difficult proposition because exterior or primary woods patinate in a continuous, long-term process. The finish, waxes, and general use contribute to color continuity in the aging surface.

If a piece has been refinished at some time in its life, especially if it is sanded in the refinishing process, all traces of exterior patina will have been removed. The object will have a glossy look and appear "good as new." In trade terminology, this piece has been "skinned" and holds little or no interest to the serious collector.

Pieces that are too perfect are suspect because any piece that has been frequently used will show signs of wear and usually scars from misuse or accidents. For example, the feet of chairs that have been dragged across the floor bear evidence of abrasion. Tilting the chair back causes rounding on the back corners of the rear feet. And if the chair leaned against the wall on a number of occasions, the upper back will show corresponding wear.

Likewise, a front stretcher placed at a convenient height for a sitter's feet shows wear, often heavy wear; chair arms are often polished smooth and the finish worn away from the grasp of many people sitting in the chair over time. For dining tables, tavern tables, and other tables with stretchers, foot wear may also be evident. Tabletops with authentic wear show all sorts of marks and abrasions, from flatware scratches to cigarette burns to food and beverage stains. If a piece was intended for everyday use, signs of wear are clearly visible.

Antique chests and cabinets should show wear in logical areas, such as around knobs and pulls. The tops of such pieces often exhibit some scratches or other discolorations. Keep in mind that wood fades from sunlight and discolors from waxes, polishes, and grime.

While purposeful frauds do turn up in the antiques market, collectors in the early 21st century are more likely to encounter pieces that were mistakenly misidentified (for example, at an estate sale) or were originally crafted as legitimate reproduction pieces.

In the United States, part of the confusion in authenticating antiques comes from the similarity between styles of 18th- and 19th-century English and American furniture because the earliest colonial cabinetmakers were often from the British Isles or had been apprenticed to British-trained artisans. The major differences between pieces crafted in England and the United States is in the use of wood. English and American furnituremakers used many of the same primary woods, but they made different choices for secondary woods. (Secondary refers to wood that is not meant to be seen, such as wood for drawer interiors, the backs of chests, and table braces.) In English-made pieces, oak was often the secondary wood; pine with notice-

able knots was also used. Because of the ready availability of virgin pine forests, American craftspeople were able to use pine known as "clear" wood—virtually free of knots. Other common secondary woods in American pieces included chestnut, poplar, and occasionally cedar. Furnituremakers in the American South also used cypress.

Another point of confusion common to both British and American furniture comes from the popularity of 18th-century furniture in the 19th century. In Britain, notable pieces of fine 18th-century furniture were copied in the first half of the 19th century. Typical pieces included dining chairs, which were divided between heirs when estates were broken up. These pieces were made by skilled artisans, and the work is comparable to that of the original pieces, making these antiques in their own right.

These early copies are rare, but late-19th-century American and English machine-made reproduction furniture is much more common. In the United States, 18th-century-style furniture made at the time of the Centennial in the 1870s is known appropriately as Centennial furniture. Although similar in appearance to 18th-century pieces, Centennial pieces are larger and have wider chair seats and taller backs. The telltale sign of Centennial pieces is the use of dowels for joinery instead of mortise-and-tenon construction.

The construction of Centennial pieces reflects technological advances. These pieces were mass-produced copies, not meant to deceive, so marks from rotary saws and modern screws and nails are easy to spot. Detailing is symmetrical and exact, reflecting the use of power tools and factory construction.

INSPIREDMIXING

A FRESH BREEZE IS BLOWING AWAY ANY REMAINING VESTIGES OF THE OLD RULES AND TRUISMS ABOUT MIXING ANTIQUES AND ART.

Starting in the mid-1980s and continuing into the

21st century, designers and architects gravitated to

the graphic punch of contemporary paintings and

mid-20th-century furniture paired with the

fine craftsmanship of 18th- and 19th-century

antiques. They found the two create a design

synergy that is a new definition of traditional style.

The tension of pairing modern with traditional feels energetic and vibrant, more visually interesting and personally expressive than the expected mix of contemporary art with 20th-century furniture or period landscapes with fine antiques.

Yet even in this free-spirited design environment, compatibility is still the key. Small pieces of art or artifacts can work with most design styles (as exotic travel souvenirs enliven English Country rooms, for example). However, the bold colors or abstract motifs of contemporary art are best set off by styles based on neoclassic Greek and Roman motifs as seen in late-18th-and early-19th-century English, European, and American furniture. Styles including English Regency; French Régence, Louis XVI, and Louis Philippe; German Biedermeier; and American Federal and Empire are noted for straight lines and neoclassic motifs, such as the eagles popular in imperial Rome and early-19th-century America. When removed from its expected environment, traditional neoclassic furniture is treated as, and seen as, sculpture.

Art in this setting is often hung gallery-style—paintings are displayed so they don't compete with each other. In a pleasing composition, a large abstract painting may fill one wall behind a low bench or above a sofa. If art pieces are hung together, they tend to be those designed for that purpose, such as studies by the same artist.

Because some of the art and furniture (large-scale Empire-style sofas, for example) are so visually commanding, design professionals and connoisseurs of this look generally favor subdued backgrounds. When antiques are paired with contemporary art in this way, plain or tailored upholstery fabrics, rather than the velvets or damasks original to the period pieces, are often the preferred design choice. Backgrounds tend to be plain, pale white walls, rather than period wall-covering, and floors left bare without rugs. Furniture and furnishings are pared down with a minimum of side tables and an absence of traditional ottomans, collections, draperies, and lamps. Lighting tends toward modern gallery-style—or a striking period chandelier hung as art.

As a variation of what is admittedly a gallerylike look, designers are also experimenting with mixing classic 20th-century furniture pieces with more traditional sofas and upholstered chairs. Because of the boldness of these designs, such rooms require the larger scale of contemporary 20th- or early-21st-century art. (Due to costs and availability, collected 19th-century and earlier art in private collections tends to be of relatively modest size; paintings are frequently stacked or otherwise grouped for a pleasing display.) When large-scale art is called for in the mix of antique and modern styles, some designers advise the playful direction of early-20th-century oil portraits, unsigned or by obscure artists, or the option of period posters. Or they may opt for black and white art photography, a staple complement to 20th-century furniture.

Other designers suggest paintings that emphasize color (as in the style of Mark Rothko or Donald Judd) to hang in rooms of American, English, or European antiques to create harmony between traditional and contemporary. Often, such paintings are hung conventionally—such as over a mantel—to relax rooms of formal antiques or new custom furniture.

Beyond well-known 19th-century antiques, art-lovers and art-loving designers are pairing 1930s and 1940s furniture, such as the glamorous mirrored styles popular in France, with the always-popular Expressionists, such as Henri Matisse, or with more conventional European landscape paintings. Owing to light finishes and curved lines, this mid-20th-century modern furniture mixes beautifully with neoclassic-style Italian and earlier French pieces.

PAGE 100: In a library updated with a raffia ceiling and Fortuny silk pendant, traditional matted drawings and a pair of pond boats stand out against the dark paneling. Furnishings include new wing chairs with contemporary lines and an Asian-inspired cube table. The black leather ottoman, in a woven design, anchors the seating arrangement and serves as a coffee table. PAGE 103: The Crosscheck bentwood chair, designed by architect Frank Gehry, leads the eye to a Portuguese-style desk and chair based on traditional designs. Regional landscape paintings appear to float on glass shelves. The red wall works as a colorful canvas for the carefully edited mix. Halogen downlights give a gallerylike ambience to the inviting retreat. PAGE 105: A bold new kilim-style wool rug serves as abstract art for the refinished vintage oak floors. The sleek wing chair, upholstered in a cashmere-and-wool blend, illustrates the classic style of updated traditional pieces. Old challis paisley covers the pillow for a punch of color and pattern. The floor lamp, a contemporary piece, reinforces the library theme while reflecting the fine lines of the more modern furnishings.

East meets West and traditional meets modern in a grandly scaled

living room that throws out any preconceptions of traditional style

in the 21st century. Here, comfort and color define the stylish mix.

ASIANINFLUENCE

Walls upholstered in a subtle moss-and-green-tea linen contrast with the graphic punch of a bold contemporary painting. The choice of one large painting, hung directly above the sofa, creates a strong focal point and immediately gives the setting the contrast of art and furnishings. Overlapping Oriental rugs infuse the room with lively color and pattern—and illustrate a playful approach to a traditional decorating element. A transitional sofa, inspired by the clean lines of English Regency furniture, anchors one of the three sitting areas in the room. The armless chair and more conventional armchair add seating and the interest of colorful fabrics. The pair of pedestal tables and the classic Chinese butterfly chair, crafted from tied raffia, allude to the Asian influences. The tie-on cushion is silk. Bright-red cloisonné lamps, in the 1960s style, top the chrome end tables.

SUBTLE LANDSCAPES

AND CHIC LAMPS

PAIR WITH A MANTEL

IN REVIVAL STYLE.

OPPOSITE: Instead of a traditional sofa or love seats, an unexpected modern classic—a reproduction 1929 Barcelona daybed designed by architect Mies van der Rohe—provides fireside seating. Contributing to the drama are a pair of contemporary bronze sculptures and an Asian-inspired accent table. The brass pharmacy-style lamp is another classic 20th-century piece, used in both contemporary and more traditional settings. BELOW: The contrast continues in the living room's third seating area, anchored by a transitional-style sofa at the window. Here, a contemporary portrait hangs next to the antique 19th-century secretary. A folding Mongolian hunting chair, a trio of antique beaded tribal hats from Africa (on the window ledge), and the rock-crystal candlesticks on the Asian-style coffee table enrich the mix. A modern candle-style globe chandelier, suspended from the Venetian-plaster ceiling, illuminates the lively scene of antiques and art.

ZenMODERN

Art for serenity, rather than pride of acquisition, sets the mood in a private sitting room designed for meditation, relaxation, and tea with a friend. The Noguchi rice-paper lantern appears to hover above.

Less is definitely more in this art lover's private sitting room, designed to be devoid of color and all but the most subtle pattern (provided by the woven sisal carpet). Here the large abstract, *Piers #7* (1998) by Alex Katz, hangs above the console tables by interior designer Thad Hayes. Ceramic vases on the console are by Berndt Friberg for Gustavsberg, Sweden. Scale gives the room its visual strength; drama emanates from striking artwork—from the sculpture, *Klee's Stone* (1982) by Isamu Noguchi and the Friberg bowl on the elliptical table, an Eames design for Herman Miller. Furnishings, restrained in their line and scale, include the Hayes-designed streamlined sofas and a club chair with shape and form as stunning as the best modern sculpture. The flowers are white calla lilies.

LAMPS DOUBLE AS ART IN A SITTING ROOM OF CHIC MODERN CLASSICS AND COMFORT.

OPPOSITE: A brass Italian easel lamp, designed by Arredoluce in the 1960s, displays and illuminates an abstract ink on paper, *Untitled, Reclining Women* (1959) by famous mid-20th-century Expressionist Willem de Kooning. The lamp style, popular in the 1950s and 1960s, works well in a room with a pared-down setting and offers an interesting alternative to more traditional floor lamps or easel-and-art displays. A halogen bulb focuses the light and provides a clear, white quality unlike the warmer tones of conventional incandescent lightbulbs. Adding to the Zenlike quality of the sitting room is the imported tea set—a black-lacquer wooden tray, a pewter teapot, and pearlescent bowls. Translucent roller shades soften the outside light. ABOVE: Giving a glamorous touch to the Zen restraint, a 1940s French lamp with a pineapple-style ceramic base is paired with the Swedish ceramics and the abstract painting. A new paper shade freshens the classic lamp and strengthens the white-on-white palette.

CREATIVETENSIONS

The contrast between modern art, Regency-

style furniture, and Art Deco accent pieces sets

up a room full of surprises and design appeal.

A living room decorated with as many styles as periods is illuminated by a grand 18th-century-style Irish crystal chandelier. Rich "espresso bean" brown walls handsomely set off the white Roman-style wall brackets that display dazzling white 17th-century French faience urns and the contemporary American color-field painting inspired by the work of Mark Rothko. The mirror is in the German Biedermeier style; the white-and-gilt console table below it is in Regency style. Contributing added contrast, white Regency-style armchairs upholstered in black vinyl are paired with a circa-1810 Regency dining table. The transitional white upholstered pieces take a turn to the glam with mink pillows, and the Art Deco-style coffee table displays a traditional tole cachepot and pair of porcelain urns.

SATURATED, HOT COLOR LEAPS FROM ESPRESSO WALLS FOR DRAMA AND FUN.

Designed for a client whose tastes run the gamut from fine European antiques to American pop culture, this living room disproves the notion that spaces with high-style antiques have to be enclaves of seriousness. The painting here, one of a pair of abstract color-field pieces, illustrates the punch of saturated color and the dramatic power of contrast. The paintings (in the style of mid-20th-century modern art) are strictly for fun, but the key furnishings, such as the round Regency table now used for cards, are high-profile pieces with impressive provenance. The mix of the two, along with the pretty polish of a traditional window treatment, guarantees a room that sizzles with energy. Well-edited accessories range from the neoclassic head to a collection of neatly stacked art books.

A 1980 abstract by Susan Doremus in shades of red hangs unframed while

certainly not unnoticed in a suburban living room full of urbane furnishings.

ARTFULDESIGN

The power of modern paintings is in their boldness in form and color and—as this presentation suggests—sometimes in their sheer size. One large, unframed canvas provides visual punch in an average size living room; furniture and accessories support without visually competing. Below the painting is a classic Eames chair, creating a gallerylike vignette. Other major pieces, such as the facing sofas and armchairs upholstered in a leaf pattern, are transitional pieces, chosen for clean lines and comfort. The pedestal table is a shared accent piece. The glass-and-iron coffee table displays the only strictly traditional element in the room: an assortment of glass inkwells assembled through years of collecting. The display of art books rotates as passions and interests shift.

OPPOSITE: A pair of armchairs are arranged for conversation and comfortable viewing of the Doremus painting. The round table between them displays a pre-Columbian figure. Wool draperies can be closed to protect the painting from direct sunlight. ABOVE: An unframed abstract Expressionist painting by Michael Nakoneczny leans on the traditional mantel, which provides a natural focal point for the striking contemporary piece. The presentation allows collectors to swap art or try a new piece without making the long-term commitment of hanging it on the wall. For a touch of green in the pristine setting, curly bamboo fills the ceramic jar. The antique Chinese dresser cabinet, which provides practical storage, adds the visual weight of its finish as well as an exotic element. A faux-leopard fabric covers the saber-leg bench, a new piece that recalls the lines of Regency-style furniture. Rather than add small tables and lamps, the designer opted for the sleek lines of the floor lamp with its classic shade. Striped pillows and the glazed cachepot, filled with seasonal flowers, contribute softer elements to the serene room of modern art and transitional furniture.

Paintings and furniture by 20th-century masters converse with antiques

in a living room where light is a crucial element of the presentation.

BAUHAUSREMEMBERED

A graphic painting by Ron Carswell over the fireplace and black leather upholstery set the powerful color palette for this art-filled living room of classic 20th-century furniture. Chrome-and-leather Barcelona chairs, designed by famed architect Mies van der Rohe, face the fireplace. The leather sofas were originally designed by Le Corbusier and are from Knoll Studio. The art quilt on the facing sofa is *The Moth* by Rae Kozai. Floating over the Heriz-pattern rug is a piece of contemporary art furniture, Josh Simpson's *Glass Balloon* table. Softening the mix of sleek contemporary furniture and large-scale modern art is a 19th-century mahogany secretary displaying a potted orchid. The bowfront chest, visible in the lower right corner, is another antique piece. The synergy of modern and traditional pieces imbues the room with a distinctly personal ambience.

A large-scale abstract painting soothes the senses in a neutral

space where artifacts from Greece, Egypt, and Africa find a home

with Regency and modern furniture and contemporary lighting.

CULTURAL MODERN

OPPOSITE: A large abstract painting by Agnes Martin graces an art lover's salon with simple, rhythmic lines across a stark white background. In the spirit of style and period diversity, a gilt-frame chaise in the 19th-century English Regency style sits beneath the painting. The upholstery fabric is velvet; pillows are silk. Arranged in the mode of seating in art museums, the chaise invites contemplation as well as conversation. The curved lines and elaborate carving offer contrast to the abstract art that hangs above. ABOVE: With raised paneling, dentil molding, and sconces as a handsome background, the designer created an artful mix of furnishings that requires no art hanging above the velvet banquette. In the spirit of symmetry, gilt and silvered screens work as foils for the contemporary tables and pair of matching lamps. Carefully chosen accessories include the Greek head and African artifacts on the table to the left. Completing the multicultural tableau, a pair of pale wood 19th-century Egyptian-style stools evoke the charms of colonial furniture. Too fragile for their original purpose, the stools now serve as coffee and drink tables.

BELOW: In a collector's salon where every element is chosen with care, the pièce de résistance is the group of log-size crystals that appear to ignite the firebox. The fire-and-ice effect is like nuggets of kryptonite, the mythical mineral that imparts power in the Superman stories. The crystals are lit from inside to suggest the warm glow of radiant heat in the coolly pristine setting. French rock-crystal sconces from the 1920s, in vogue again, continue the effect, flanking the traditional mantel. Carefully arranged for an altar effect, a table displays cylindrical Egyptian alabaster vessels and African artifacts. A low table covered with a rug serves multiple functions—from displaying orchids for parties and receptions to doubling as an informal dining table for family and close friends. The quilted floor pillows are silk.

OPPOSITE: In the milieu of global design, the salon's handsome traditional architecture serves as the stage for the disparate furnishings and artifacts that capture the owner's imagination. Making everything coalesce in serene harmony is the neutral palette, including the gauze-and-taffeta draperies, which abstain from obvious color and pattern. Cowhide rugs bleached white introduce hints of texture and organic shape over the white area rug. The unusual African shell money rings stand on the mantel, as beautiful as sculpture and particularly arresting without the competition of other pieces. Adding scale, the oversize globe turns on a paw-foot stand crafted to recall 19th-century style. A simple armless chair on casters unites the elements of the room and balances the artifact-laden table on the other side.

THE MIX MASTERED

Contemporary art is the start for two living rooms—one in soft earth tones, the other in

primary colors—that successfully balance a mix of furniture, materials, styles, and periods.

In both rooms, art and tasteful display are the rules of the modernist design game.

OPPOSITE: An unmistakably modern painting, *Superintelligence* by Jeffrey Lewis, sparks a scheme of unexpected color and inventive pairings. The art unifies the seemingly unrelated elements, including a reproduction 18th-century-style Spanish Colonial table with heavy caning and an Edward Wormley-inspired chaise covered in a lavender hue taken from the painting. The shade repeats as table accessory, as upholstery for the Moderne-style chrome-base stools, and as a chaise pillow. Lamp bases are a contemporary interpretation of 19th-century mercury glass. The lamps give definition to the long table and direct attention to the painting. ABOVE: A painting by French artist Roger Muhl above the classic parsons table initiates a quiet, earthy scheme for a contemporary living room. The stools under the table are in a Wormley design from the 1950s. The chaise is a tête-à-tête sofa after a Wormley design, and the pillows are wool with mohair trim. Accessories include gongs on stands, marble urns, and round wooden boxes.

ABOVE: A striking acrylic-on-paper by Portland, Oregon, artist Angelita Surman hangs above a heavily carved French pine console in the foyer of an art-filled home, hinting at the visual pleasures to come. Sculptural topiaries enhance the bold lines of the artwork and add verticality to the grouping. In keeping with the symmetry of pairs, ivory balls on stands flank the flower-filled rose bowl, and upholstered pillow-top stools tuck under the circa-1850 console. OPPOSITE: Current contemporary art, such as *Two Clouds*, an April Gornik charcoal drawing, flanked by electrified candle sconces, enlivens a dining room of neoclassic-style furniture. The English marble-top rosewood console features a rare Wedgwood plaque in the center of the table skirt. (This important piece dates from 1790.) The dining chairs are reproductions crafted in the style of 18th-century Swedish neoclassic pieces.

A contemporary painting by Nathlie Suzanne dramatizes a grandly-scaled dining room designed to evoke the casual elegance of Barbados. The scale of such contemporary art balances the ceiling height of this late-18th-century house and creates a warm, relaxed ambience. Colorful draperies hang from iron rods inspired by the artist's French heritage; paired with the white walls, they lighten the look of the British Colonial-style custom table and reproduction chairs. Rather than turn the room into a gallery or historic reproduction, the owners opted for a lighter, fresher approach, with only the major painting above an antique console, a handpainted screen for decoration, and a reproduction painted-iron-and-crystal chandelier. Vintage antelope horns introduce an offbeat element into the space.

OPPOSITE: A color-field painting by contemporary artist Louis Bunce revs up the color palette in the sunroom of this circa-1912 home. In keeping with the Pacific Coast location of the home, antique Chinese children's chairs contribute Asian influences to the mix—and strengthen the red palette. Celadon green vases on the mantel infuse the room with the energy of contrast. Acorn finials and black iron urns complete the artfully arranged tableau, which can be changed with the seasons or the homeowners' whims. ABOVE: Propped against the wall in the style of 19th-century pier mirrors, a contemporary painting initiates a neutral color scheme in the living room. The drama of the large piece likewise gives the classic vignette of a chair, floor lamp, and side table an interesting twist and provides a stunning, unexpected focal point to the room. Multiplying interest are the updated take on the classic butler's tray and the faux-zebra fabric on the oversize ottoman that serves as a coffee table. The parsons table to the left, lacquered white, is a modern classic.

Good work bears repeating. Imitation is the sincerest form of flattery.

So why the conundrum about using reproduction furniture pieces?

THE GREAT DEBATE

Applied to the fabulous furniture of centuries and periods past, these sentiments have fueled the reproduction of fabulous case and upholstered goods whose original production has ceased. How wonderful that one can enjoy such things as baroque and neoclassical design in a modern-day home. While there are those who turn up their noses at the idea of having anything but the original, others, including such notable names as Thomas Jefferson, believe that good design and beauty should be widely present and available. And while many people who love antiques adore the hunt, the thrill of landing a rare find, some of those beautiful antique originals are outrageously expensive or simply no longer available. The availability of the reproduction pieces we adore saves us from pouting in the corner, giving us options other than unrequited longing for an Empire sideboard that we can't find or afford.

But how do you choose well? What makes a good reproduction? To the first question, interior designer Marshall Watson of New York City suggests heading to the museums—as often as you can—for an inexpensive, but very effective visual education. "In museums you'll see the best examples of the originals as they are now," says Watson. "You'll become familiar with the details, the scale, and proportion of styles that you love. The surfaces have such patina, a subtle quality that develops with time and use."

As for what makes a good reproduction, the answer is, to a degree, subjective. Is it complete adherence to physical size, scale, and proportion as well as to materials, composition, and construction method? Should the finished piece resemble the original as it would be freshly produced, or should it resemble the original as it is now? "If you're accustomed to antiques, the "new" look of some reproduction pieces can feel a little shiny or jarring," cautions Watson. Certainly these fresh reproductions will develop patina over time, but it's not something that happens quickly, and it is worth noting when buying a reproduction. Alternatively, craftsmen now have the tools and finish techniques to turn out handsome reproduction pieces that, placed next to the originals, make it difficult to iden tify which is which. To some, artificial aging makes a reproduction piece seem forced and less acceptable; others wouldn't have a reproduction any other way. There is no right or wrong answer, of course, it's a subjective matter of what you like and will enjoy.

The best museum furniture-reproduction programs are super-vised by curators and historians who have much to offer with respect to historical accuracy and give us a look at the reproduc-tion process. For example, when a piece is chosen for repro-duction at Colonial Williamsburg, the manufacturer's furni-ture designer works directly from the orig-inal piece at Colonial Williamsburg, starting with the creation of a detailed, full-size drawing. Plastic molds are made of carving and relief details, such as ball and claw feet and cabriole legs, to ensure accurate repli-cation. Drawings and molds are then pre-sented to the Colonial Williamsburg Product Review Committee; acceptable substitutions are discussed and determined at that point. "If a piece was originally crafted in apple wood but that's no longer available," explains Kristen Fischer, the foundation's director of licensing for furniture and tabletop works, "we might choose another fruitwood—particularly if the piece might have existed as such originally."

Fischer's example of making a piece in an alternate wood—because the original is no

longer available—brings up the issue of conces-sions made in reproduction furniture: what, why, and when are modifications permissible. The review board of museum curators and historians tackle all of these in the production process, as does any maker of high-quality reproduction pieces. There are primary woods (visible exter-nally), and secondary woods (used internally). And a long list of questions are discussed at length. For example: Must one duplicate both, or just the primary woods? Should original join-ery and construction methods be replaced with modern methods if the latter is more cost efficient or more durable? How should the piece be finished if original substances are no longer available or are now illegal? What aspects of reproduc-tion do buyers appreci-ate and are they willing to pay for?

The goal of the Colonial Williamsburg Foundation is to create pieces that physically appear to match the original 18th-century antiques they are copied from, as closely as possible, while using modern finishes and techniques. The entire process requires six to 12 months before an approved prototype stands next to the orig-inal for a side-by-side review before production begins. "Our reproductions are always in a finish approximating a new 18th-century piece," Fischer explains of Colonial Williamsburg's reproduction pieces, and the philosophy is not to artificially age a piece. The program often allows modern interior construction methods, such as joinery, because it is superior to earlier methods and, as such, will last longer and stand up to years of everyday use. The lesson here is to know that variables exist and to decide what is important to you.

Within the Colonial Williamsburg program, pieces identified as reproductions are line-for-line copies of the original. In fact, select pieces are copied down to the very square-nail style originally used. Those identified as adaptations of originals are a very close match but with scale and proportion changes made to accommodate current users. (Be aware that there is no standard vernacular. In the offerings of other high-quality reproduction furniture makers, you will find pieces marked "reproduction" that have actually been adapted for modern-day users. Be sure to ask.) For example, as a people we're bigger than people who sat in dining chairs 200 years ago. Our legs are longer and our derrieres are wider, and it simply wouldn't make sense to sit in a chair made for smaller folk. Similarly, our homes are larger and many historic furnishings have been adapted to include taller backs to suit the scale of rooms with higher ceilings. Another variation of reproduction pieces, called interpretations, also are produced by the Colonial Williamsburg program. "These pieces are generally things that consumers are looking for and they're reminiscent of the Colonial Williamsburg period." Colonial Williamsburg is diligent in its use of these terms—reproduction, adaptation, interpretation—commonly used by other makers as well. Still, it can't be emphasized strongly enough that these terms don't mean the same thing from one maker to the other. A reputable maker should

welcome your inquiry as to the differences between the piece in question and its original.

Museum programs are not the only source of quality reproduction furniture, and for some buyers, museum standards are either too inflexible or too flexible, or the offerings too limited. There are fabulous furniture makers turning out faithful, finely crafted reproduction pieces in the United States and abroad. Similarly, skilled artisans in custom shops across the country will gladly produce an exact copy of your coveted piece, matching composition, construction to near-clone level—or conversely, will work with you to produce a piece to whatever standards you set but to suit your modern-day purpose (media storage, for example) and dimensions.

It's worth noting that mass-market merchants have tapped our love for historic design forms as well. Mall shops and franchise retailers offer pieces from the most popular historic design periods. Of course it's best to consider these to be made in the style of their period rather than reproductions or adaptations; the visual education that you've gleaned from seeing authentic originals will tell you this immediately. That said, these mass-market works are often better looking than you might initially expect; they're not costly and can fill a need. We all have to furnish our homes with something, and if $500 is what we have to spend on a desk or coffee table, well, we should have options.

Ultimately, the question of what makes a good reproduction, adaptation, or interpretation comes back to you, the buyer. If you believe the sideboard or desk or table you've just brought home is beautiful and worth what you paid for it, then it's good. If its composition and construction and modifications square with what you want, then it's good. Moreover, do you love using it, seeing it, living with it. Do you take pleasure in its history; the effort and craftsmanship that made it possible to have it in your home? Enough said.

There's another wrinkle to consider: Some pieces have been reproduced over time and have themselves become respectable antiques or vintage pieces. After all, the concept of reproduction furniture is hardly new. "It was very popular in the 1880s to the turn of the last century to revive certain periods, reproducing works from the 18th century," explains Marshall Watson. These reproductions—in a twist, now antiques themselves—are referred to as centennial pieces. Ironically, quite affordable solutions in some cases are the reproductions crafted in the 1940s and '50s, as many pieces produced then have now developed the much sought-after patina of age and resemble the antique originals.

Watson cites the example of the classic Pembroke table, a 4-legged small, rectangular table with a drawer and two drop leaves that when raised, form an oval top. "These were reproduced quite accurately by the thousands in the '40s," he explains, "and now can be had for prices ranging from $800 to $2,000." By comparison, a good current reproduction of the same table will run anywhere from $4,000 to $7,000; a 150-year-old version for $5,000; and

if you want an original 18th-century Pembroke, you'll pay $12,000 to $35,000.

Modern furniture is experiencing a similar situation. Pay attention if you're buying mid-20th-century furniture. Many of the classics—Mies van der Rohe's Barcelona chair and ottoman, the Eames molded plywood chair and Eames lounge chair, LeCorbuier's fabulous leather-and-chromed steel chaise longue—are still in production. So what might appear to be reproductions are actually knock-offs, which must be altered enough not to infringe on the original's copyright. If you can, buy originals from the authorized manufacturer. They'll reward you with beauty and value.

In a particular instance, there's one piece of furniture that is best chosen in reproduction form, interior designers agree: It's the dining chair. It's a piece that must withstand considerable wear and activity, and it must fit! A comfortable dining chair for someone sitting at a table 200 years ago was considerably smaller than one that suits our larger, taller, wider bodies today. "Antique chairs can't withstand heavy use for long: The wood is dry, the glue is brittle; they will break eventually," says Watson, "and they'll break your heart. Best to go with good reproductions."

Still undecided? Take a moment to ponder Marshall Watson's comment: "A professor once told me that 'a reproduction was all but the essence of a piece. That said, when someone makes 12 dining chairs to put around a table—which is the original and which are the copies—and which is better?'".

PRESENTATION OF ART

THE ART OF DISPLAY

THE ARRANGEMENT AND DISPLAY OF ART AND ANTIQUES CONTRIBUTE TO HOW THEY ARE VIEWED, ENJOYED, AND CONSERVED.

With sparer styles and multicultural influences,

collectors focus on individual pieces in simple

settings. As lighting and presentation play major

roles, the demise of heavy window treatments

also exposes pieces to sun damage. For coverage,

screens, shades, or window films are used and

give the look of, little or no window covering.

Although more is never too much for passionate collectors, less can be more when it comes to effective display. Antique English tea caddies, small French bronze sculptures, or Chinese mudmen look charming arranged in ample numbers or mixed with leather-bound books in built-ins. But packed shelves and crowded tabletops can spoil the desired effect and look messy and obsessive.

To avoid overcrowding and overwhelming a room, designers advise their collector clients to rotate items, perhaps bringing out collections or parts of collections seasonally. Serious collectors often overcome the problem by regularly trading up, swapping lesser antiques or art for finer pieces as their eye and resources improve.

To design a room around a collection or incorporate a collection into the overall scheme, interior designers advocate grouping like objects, adding built-ins if necessary for neatness, and creating a natural focal point. Any collection, from small and modest to extensive and grand, looks more important when like objects are grouped. If the collection is extensive enough (such as leather-bound books, small drawings, or a particular kind of porcelain) it frequently requires a combination of wall surfaces and adjacent built-ins or étagères and tabletops. (Caveat: If the room is relatively modest in size, an extensive collection will be more pleasingly presented if it is the only one present. Two or more extensive collections in a small space creates the ambience of a shop or museum.)

Collections can be easily arranged on shelves or tabletops, but wall displays often prove more challenging. The best advice from designers and galleries is the simplest: Hang the most important artwork where it is most visible and most enjoyed. In practice, this translates to hanging art at seated eye level. The natural tendency is often to hang art too high, especially in rooms with 10-foot or higher ceilings. With high, sometimes soaring, ceilings often the norm in newer houses, designers may incorporate tall vertical elements, such as cartoons—wall drawings with the patterns copied from tapestries—that fit the scale of such spaces. Other options when dealing with high ceilings include stacking paintings rather than scattering them around the room, or installing a picture rail that allows for the rotation of framed, wire-hung art.

Built-ins, freestanding bookcases, or étagères solve the problem of overly crowded tabletops. Adjustable shelves are a reasonable option for collectors, particularly for those who are likely to swap out items of varying sizes. If heavy books are to be part of the display or are the primary collection, each shelf span requires reinforcement every 28 inches to avoid sagging. Picture lighting, added to the exteriors of built-ins, gives a pleasing gallery feel to a room where at least one wall is floor-to-ceiling shelves.

Art and collections work well when displayed as a natural focal point—such as over the mantel—or grouped on the most prominent wall as a primary or secondary focal point. A favorite painting or cherished family portrait is an obvious and pleasing choice over a mantel; a creative arrangement may incorporate brackets for display. Used in this manner, brackets flank or surround a mirror, artwork, or a part of the collection. Other important pieces may be displayed on the mantel.

In a room without a mantel, such as a dining room, the longest wall may serve as the primary focal point. A large painting or screen that fits the scale of the room is a logical choice; alternatively a grid of paintings, drawings, or prints or a collection may fill the space.

A generously sized foyer or entrance or upstairs hall may work well to display collections of neatly arranged artwork, such as prints or art photographs. Likewise, the stairwell, particularly when open to the entrance hall, provides a stunning setting for groups of collected paintings or drawings, such as antique botanical prints or small oil paintings. An upstairs hall connecting family bedrooms or a private back stairwell from bedrooms to the kitchen is ideal for grouping framed family photographs, new or vintage.

PAGE 142: The circular motifs of the abstract art repeat in the antique demilune table and the carved detail on the back of the antique chair. PAGE 145: Custom wallcovering depicting a 19th-century map of Paris serves as wall-size art and provides a textured background for the sleek metallic-finish chest; the chairs are French antiques; the gilded opaline chinoiserie vases also are antique. PAGE 147: Hung almost floor-to-ceiling, prints of sections of a Paris map are grouped as a striking backdrop for 1920s French chairs. Gilt frames dress up the map prints, repeating the golden tones of the metal chairs. A 1940s chandelier, crafted from Venetian glass, reinforces the glamorous setting. A grid arrangement of evenly spaced prints or paintings combines the impact of a large-scale piece of art, such as modern painting, with the interest of multiple pieces. Presentation is key: Use a series of prints or artwork with some common theme, such as small landscapes from the same school of art, and identical matting and framing.

Designed as obelisks of display, two matching hand-carved bookcases

work double duty in a small city apartment, neatly storing magazines and

artfully displaying plates, shells, and favorite decorative accessories.

STYLE DISPLAYED

Presentation is everything in an artfully designed living room of a city apartment. Setting the scene is the sofa, skirted in the style of famous decorator Syrie Maugham. The obelisk-shaped bookcases are another ode to a design legend, inspired by a pair attributed to decorator Nancy Lancaster, neatly organizing magazines, shells, and collected treasures. In the tight confines of the city-size living room, the obelisk shape turns utilitarian and necessary storage into sculpture—and avoids the blocky look of more conventional bookcases and the space-grabbing quality of built-ins. On the shelves, the arrangement of objects in pairs—plates on stands, small obelisks, and elevated mosaic balls—contributes to the orderly display. The Regency-style bamboo chair and the hand-carved, hand-painted floor lamp add to the stylish tableaux.

BELOW: In a light-filled sunroom illuminated by a grand rock-crystal chandelier, careful grouping provides a soothing ambience and gives continuity to the setting. Pairing imparts order to the stacked prints and the staggered brackets displaying metal crosses in the music corner. OPPOSITE: Stacked antique botanical engravings, identically matted and decoratively framed, harmonize with the serene neutral decor. The unframed painting by Bernd Haussmann freshens the setting with an unexpected contemporary touch. In this monochromatic scheme, the collection of cream and white china offers a subtle interplay of shapes. Silver frames in a variety of styles unify five generations of family photographs on a tole table, showing the impact of grouping. The woven basket on the shelf below is an African tribal piece, an unexpected touch that attests to the owner's love of travel.

OPPOSITE: A traditional family portrait takes on a more contemporary look when hung adjacent to an undraped floor-length window. The size of the oil painting, by 20th-century American artist Lydia Field Emmett, ensures its focal-point status in a handsomely furnished living room. The brass light adds a nighttime glow to the burnished surface of the portrait. Grouped for effect, Edwardian silver boxes share the top of the Regency tea table with an antique bowl on rosewood stand. The antique sofa, covered in yellow damask, is in Chippendale style. BELOW: Hung from sofa top to ceiling, a staggered grid arrangement offers a creative solution for displaying collected contemporary art. Matching black frames and identical matting pull the graphic art together, multiplying the dramatic impact. In contrast to the contemporary art, a matching pair of tole lamps on antique side tables and a traditional Staffordshire-print pillow fabric introduce 19th-century English sensibilities into the personal mix.

Hand-carved brackets mounted on tongue-and-groove paneling present antique Chinese exportware grouped around a sunburst mirror. The display increases the visual importance of the symmetrically arranged porcelain and offers a safe way to enjoy the fine collection. Platters and plates fill in to complete the vignette. A 19th-century Dutch marble-top commode holds a pair of lamps fabricated from circa-1870 porcelain vases. The border of the Flemish paper screen with a charming pastoral scene repeats the blues of the exportware. With the wall arrangement as the focal point, the mantel offers a simpler scene: a rose medallion platter below a Venetian mirror.

ABOVE: The combined living room/library of a suburban Paris townhouse aptly illustrates the French penchant for combining the practical with the decorative. Simple wall-mounted shelves, covered in printed cotton to match the walls, store books. The wall below displays collected prints. In this personal setting, family photographs in silver frames are grouped on the antique secretary. OPPOSITE: Built-in bookshelves and a mantel, the ever-classic venues for displays, neatly contain a mix of elements. Lower shelves pull utilitarian duty, corralling magazines too interesting to toss. In this collector's home, a fine 19th-century trumeau mirror, flanked by electrified candle sconces and engravings, imbues the room with formality. As a counterpoint to the serious decorative elements, the mantel displays an ever-changing vignette of favored objects, such as the pair of obelisks, seasonal flowers, cards, and invitations.

OPPOSITE, CLOCKWISE FROM TOP LEFT: A 19th-century American Empire mahogany secretary elevates a pond boat, a toy that has gained status as a desirable collectible. The simplicity of Empire furniture showcases such sculptural decorative accessories well. In a sunroom, two pairs of engravings decorate the narrow wall space between French doors; an antique armillary sphere alludes to the room's subtle garden theme. A classic secretary displays a fine collection of antique majolica, antique leatherbound books, and family photographs. A collection of religious art, including statues of Christian saints, graces a neoclassic-style chest. A scrolled iron stand to the left displays a religious painting. The hall chair is 19th-century English. ABOVE: In an inviting sitting room, walls covered in a floral fabric and detailed with braided trim provide the visual interest and energy of an allover printed backdrop. Rather than compete with the pair of traditional landscape engravings, the floral offers the interest of color and pattern. The contrasting blue-and-white floral chair with a leopard-print pillow introduces unexpected accents. The antique painted book cabinet keeps volumes handy.

ABOVE: Unframed contemporary landscape paintings by California artist Wade Hoefer are grouped in a neat grid above a new mahogany étagère inspired by an 18th-century French antique. The open étagère displays a collection of 19th-century wooden boxes. The reproduction caned armchair re-creates the look of a British Colonial piece. OPPOSITE, CLOCKWISE FROM TOP LEFT: A large landscape by Danish painter Peder Monsted hangs above a contemporary console, which serves as a foil for an array of traditional decorative objects, including a pair of candelabra. Below the console, prints lean against the wall for extra display. Stacked art allows a collector to enjoy personal favorites in the bedroom; a modern piece hangs on the adjacent wall. A Victorian burnt-bamboo hall rack with a mirror and hooks finds new life as an easel for landscape paintings that add charm to a small bedroom; the wall-hung painting above it completes the arrangement. In a sophisticated living room, wall plaques with European harvest motifs pair with a neoclassic-style marble-top console table. The repetition of the gilded detailing links the highly decorative elements. The blue-and-white porcelain lamp gives cool visual relief.

ABOVE: In an upstairs hall, blue mats on a lively blue-and-white toile wallcovering freshen a trio of Currier and Ives lithographs in antique frames. The prints, which depict idealized scenes of 19th-century American life, are increasingly popular due to a growing interest in the furniture and decorative arts of the period. The grandfather clock, chest, and hall chairs are English antiques. OPPOSITE: Excess reigns in the dining room of a collector's suburban Paris townhouse. Printed cotton fabric used as wallcovering amplifies the collection of blue-and-white porcelain that decorates the étagère and armoire, and graces the dining table. Pieces range from fine 18th- and 19th-century Chinese exportware to 20th-century reproductions found at flea markets. The collection takes on a creative life of its own as cups, saucers, and vases detail the custom chandelier. Detailed, colored depictions of butterflies, in brass-trimmed frames, create the layered look of late-19th-century interiors.

OPPOSITE: Rooms with the grand scale of high ceilings, wainscoting, and ornate mantels offer a perfect milieu for fine art. In this French living room with stylized leaf-motif wallpaper, the ceiling height allows two large ornately framed French landscapes to be stacked above the marble mantel. Smaller pieces hang at a lower height for easy viewing; oval pieces are arranged together for unity. A second pair of large paintings is displayed above the sofa. In a symmetrical arrangement favored in French decor, a pair of antique porcelain urns anchors the mantel; small sculptures stand between the hurricane candle globes. BELOW: An open botanical pattern strikes a dramatic theme as the backdrop for a collection of matted botanical prints. The wall print repeats on the upholstered bed, coverlet, shams, dust ruffle, and chair (far right), illustrating that a theme set by the art can be an interesting starting point for an entire room. This one-note decorating might be restrictive in a more public space such as a living room, where mixing styles is often desirable, but the botanical mood feels soothing and serene in a master or guest bedroom.

CARE & CONSERVATION

PRESERVATION ENSURES THAT TREASURES FROM ONE GENERATION ARE SAVED FOR THE NEXT.

Acquisition and ownership of fine art and antiques

carries with it responsibilities: everyday care, sound

conservation, and in some cases proper professional

restoration of fragile pieces. Art and antiques are

purchased to be enjoyed, but they are also trusts—

to be valued and passed down to family or to

appropriate institutions that enrich the public.

Proper care of art and antiques begins with appropriate professional restoration, if necessary, followed by thoughtful conservation and routine care. For both antique furniture and art, routine measures, such as constant temperature and humidity and protection from direct sunlight, are key factors in preservation.

The care of art begins with proper framing techniques. Galleries that sell original art, whatever its provenance, provide framing expertise to appropriately incorporate art into its intended setting. Some rules have relaxed, but, in general, oil and acrylic paintings, except for the smallest works, are framed without mat or glass. This allows the texture to be part of the visual experience. Worn, dirty, or damaged paintings require professional restoration. Museums and galleries are sources of names of art restorers. Except for light routine dusting of the painting with a soft, dry, clean paintbrush, leave all other care to professionals. Water or cleaning or dusting sprays should never be used to clean a painting. When in doubt, consult a professional restorer or an art gallery.

Likewise, dust the ornate picture frames sometime used to enhance oil paintings with a clean, dry, soft paintbrush. Pure canned air without lubricants or cleaners, available through computer and art supply stores, works well for the most decorative art—and mirror—frames. The attachable, strawlike nozzle can be used to reach small cracks and crevices.

Watercolors, prints, drawings, etchings, lithographs, photographs, and woodblocks are traditionally matted and framed with glass. Mats should be archival and acid-free to avoid damaging the art; never allow the glass to touch the art. If the back of a print or drawing is torn or the mat damaged, it should be professionally cleaned, rematted, and reframed.

Acrylic shadow boxes, often backed with a textured fabric such as linen, offer a safe method for displaying small art objects or artifacts. Professional conservation framing is required for proper protection.

All artwork, including tapestries, textiles, and other needlework, should be hung on walls protected from direct sun, heat, cooking, and smoke. Also, prevent extreme swings in temperature and humidity. Maintain the humidity at 45 to 50 percent and the temperature a constant 65 to 68 degrees.

As with art, furniture should be protected from direct sun and extreme swings in temperature and humidity. Regular dusting is the key to proper care. Effective weekly dusting removes dust particles that cause scratches. Experts advocate dusting with a very slightly damp, clean, soft cotton cloth or a lamb's-wool duster that contains lanolin. (The dusters are effective for reaching carved or turned areas that are hard to reach with a cloth.)

Lemon oil or other furniture oils or products that contain silicone or synthetic materials are not recommended for fine antique wood furniture. Likewise, do not use water or solvents to clean furniture. Damaged finishes require professional restoration. Valuable antiques or treasured family pieces also should be professionally restored.

Normal care for antiques in good condition includes weekly dusting plus yearly waxing with a professional furniture wax. Before waxing furniture, dust it with a dusting or static cloth. Quality furniture wax is formulated from beeswax and carnauba wax. It should be applied with a clean, soft cotton cloth and allowed to dry before buffing with clean, rolled-up cheesecloth.

To polish hardware, first remove it from the furniture piece, then clean the piece with a brass cleaner and buff it dry. When hardware is cleaned on the furniture, the cleaner may leave a halo effect.

When a piece has been overwaxed, you can safely clean it with a professional-quality buildup remover applied with #0000 (very fine) steel wool, working in the direction of the grain. Depending on how much sun exposure a piece receives, the finish may be revived every 12-18 months with a restoration product, such as Howard Restor-A-Finish. If a piece receives frequent exposure to sun, direct light, or heat, products such as Howard Orange Oil or Feed-N-Wax beeswax will help prevent drying and cracking.

PAGE 166: When the care of a piece of art isn't compromised, rules are made to be broken. Artist Eric Fischl insisted that his painting, inspired by a visit to Rome, be left unframed. Below the painting is a late-18th-century gilded console table. PAGE 169: An antique gilded Italian frame pairs with a new painting by Todd Murphy. The juxtaposition of old and new creates a striking display. PAGE 171: Brass picture lights are a traditional method to illuminate a fine painting. Although professionally designed and installed lighting is an option for serious collectors, picture lights are charming alternatives to more elaborate methods. The picture light sets a period scene appropriate to *The Courier* (1912), an oil painting by illustrator N.C. Wyeth. The North Carolina walnut sideboard below displays a Charleston bracket clock and a Confederate cavalry officer's saber with the original sash.

Collectors balance daily enjoyment of art, collections, and antiques

with the requirements of caring for and preserving their treasures.

STYLEPRESERVED

OPPOSITE: Although museum settings avoid heat and direct sunlight, the mantel is the classic display in the home for treasured art, such as *Ides of March* (1974) by Andrew Wyeth, in a paneled library. Such indirect heat from a properly designed fireplace is usually safe unless a painting is extremely fragile. However, checking with a conservator is recommended. Here, because the fireplace is used infrequently, the collector chose the traditional display of his treasure. ABOVE: Although more stable and less subject to fading than color photography, protect black-and-white prints from direct sunlight as well as extreme swings in temperature and humidity. Negatives should always be saved and stored for black-and-white as well as color family portraits and special-occasion photography so that new prints can be made if necessary.

OPPOSITE: Art is paramount in this paneled library that doubles as a dining room for dinner parties. The raised paneling visually frames the oil painting and the smaller works on paper. Recessed ceiling lighting contributes to the gallerylike ambience. The painting over the mantel is *On the Beach* (1964) by Yugoslavian artist Gustav Likan. The artist became well-known in the United States as director of the Chicago Academy of Fine Art. The sculpture on the dining table is *The Dancer* by Romain de Tirtoff-Erté; it is based on an Erté painting. BELOW: Dining rooms provide ideal environments for art, normally featuring an interior wall away from direct sunlight and often uninterrupted space for larger works, such as this dramatic diptych by Fayue Jones. The high-impact piece is a sophisticated departure from the more commonly seen landscapes or portraits that often grace dining room walls. The colorful work is a pleasing segue to the contemporary glass-top dining table and recovered upholstered chairs from the 1970s. The crystal chandelier refines the setting and casts a soft nighttime glow on the art.

OPPOSITE: Whether prized by collectors with interests in history or treasured as family heirlooms, portraits are worthy of care and conservation. Because of the interest in portraiture in 18th- and 19th-century Europe and the United States, portrait paintings are readily available for the collector. Depending on where a portrait was purchased or stored, expert cleaning and restoration may be required. Antiques dealers, art galleries that specialize in period art, and art museums can provide names of restorers. In this room of American antiques, a portrait hangs above a mantel displaying collected silver Jefferson cups. ABOVE: A stylized painting of a woman done in a contemporary tone hangs in a living room that mixes styles and periods. Hung frameless, the canvas is a dramatic counterpoint to the striking black-and-white photographs leaning against the mantel. White mats with simple black frames, the classic presentation for photography, illustrate the importance of allowing the art to star. The pair of photographs works well in the horizontal space and can be easily changed out with other pieces from the owners' collection.

OPPOSITE: An upstairs study provides the perfect milieu for a room devoted to the owner's passion for prints. Hung on an interior wall, the prints are protected from direct sunlight. Archival matting and framing ensures proper care and longevity. Bookcases hold a variety of art books and references. As with art, fine books should be stored in an environment with controlled temperature and humidity. Regular dusting also helps preserve fine volumes. BELOW: In an art-lover's living room, butterscotch walls provide a warm backdrop that doesn't compete with the works on paper. The directional ceiling lighting, from a professional lighting consultant, emphasizes the art in gallery fashion. The large piece in the center is a Pablo Picasso linoleum cut, *Jacqueline Reading* (1964). Works on paper to the immediate left are Henri Matisse's *Petite Aurore* (1923) and Picasso's *Four Children Viewing a Monster* (1934). To the right are Salvador Dalí's *Les Chants de Maldoror* (1934) and *City of Drawers* (1957). The sculpture on the Asian-influenced coffee table is a figurative work by Francisco Zungia (1969), an artist from Costa Rica and Mexico. Art and travel books displayed on the lower shelf, family snapshots on a side table, and a collection of crystal candlesticks contribute personal touches.

OPPOSITE: Antique tapestries, such as this beautifully preserved Belgian antique, contribute the scale and presence required by grandly proportioned rooms of traditional art and antiques. Often more fragile than paintings, antique tapestries require professional conservation and careful display. Here, the tapestry is displayed on an interior wall, away from direct sunlight. Picture lights, professionally chosen for the tapestry, softly illuminate the subtle texture. On the adjacent wall, a halogen-strip picture light casts pure light on the 18th-century religious painting. The trio of mezzotint prints are also antiques. The lamps, table clock, and urn are neoclassic accents that play off the motif set by the pilasters with Corinthian capitals. ABOVE: In a pretty bedroom, an antique French screen finds new purpose behind an upholstered headboard. Originally designed to define spaces, create privacy, or control drafts, screens serve admirably as art. Wall-mounted installation protects screens from the possible damage if a floor screen is accidentally toppled. As with paintings and tapestries, painted screens fare better when protected from sudden, dramatic changes in temperature and humidity and from direct sunlight and heat. In this bedroom, the louvered shutters block harsh afternoon sun. Signs of age add character to antique screens, but damaged or fragile screens should be professionally conserved to prevent further deterioration.

OPPOSITE: Coveted by interior designers and collectors, mirrors are valued for their frames as well as their reflecting abilities. This French trumeau mirror, found in New Orleans and flanked by antique metal sconces, is a fine example of the painted detail associated with such pieces. Originally crafted in the late 18th century in the Louis XV and XVI styles, trumeau mirrors were popular into the 19th century. The characteristic element is a painted scene, often pastoral, or a carved, highly decorative panel above the mirror. As with all antiques, original trumeau mirrors (frame and mirror) are more prized and valuable than repaired or altered examples.
ABOVE: Tilted down to reflect a beautifully appointed living room, a large antique French mirror adds drama to the setting. The ornate gilded frame, with an oval mirror and swag-and-urn detail, is a stunning piece of period art and a fine example of French decorative arts. Fine mirrors require special care. They should never be sprayed to clean. Rather, remove spots or dust with a clean, lint-free, soft cotton cloth, lightly dampened with water or mild glass cleaner.

OPPOSITE: Popular in the United States since colonial times, blue-and-white porcelains continue to be manufactured in Asian countries for export. The porcelains are sometimes called exportware because they were originally manufactured in China to be exported to Europe and the American colonies. As with any porcelain, safe display, such as this overdoor pediment, ensures that pieces won't be broken or cracked. Cracks and breaks require professional porcelain restoration; repairs with a commercial glue from a hardware store will lower the value of a piece. BELOW: A carved overmantel from England displays Imari porcelains. A classic accompaniment to traditional decor in England and the United States, Imari porcelains date to 17th-century Japan and China. Through the Dutch East India Company, Europeans developed a taste for the densely patterned, red, blue, and gold porcelains. Eventually, porcelain factories in Germany, France, and England copied the palette and patterns. Japanese Imari came back into fashion in 19th-century Victorian America after Commodore Matthew Perry engineered a treaty that opened Japanese trade. In the late 20th century, Imari was popular again, as part of the revival of the English-Country house look.

OPPOSITE, CLOCKWISE FROM TOP LEFT: In an entry of a country house, botanical prints hang below sconce-flanked metal wall art. A dramatically lit alcove serves as a mini art gallery for a collection of black-and-white architectural photographs. Chosen for their striking compositions, the photos surround an 1820s tall-case clock. A contemporary painting, *Deux Femmes* (1974) by Jacques Boeri, pairs with a 19th-century sculpture, *Figure on a Goat* (1897) by Paul Peterich displayed on a brown-lacquered chest. With blue walls for contrast, *Flags at Sea* (1997) by Andrew Wyeth hangs above the circa 1830 Georgia-made huntboard, a plantation piece also known as a slab. The desk below, New York circa 1800, is a miniature with rolltop, part of a collection of miniature furniture. ABOVE: Academic drawings from an extensive collection of 19th-century French and Italian works on paper are displayed at eye level below the antique candle sconces. The archival mats and delicate gilded frames unify smaller drawings, such as the piece hung to the far right, with the larger pieces in the collection. The gilded armchairs are 19th-century Italian; the starburst table base relaxes the serious pieces with a playful touch.

Knowing the terms and key words makes all the difference in understanding the language of art and antiques. Words and phrases from many countries and time periods meld into one as the collector and devotee begins to speak and communicate in this meaningful language.

REFERENCE. ABSTRACT ART. Paintings and other media made up of color and form, not recognizable objects; identified with the 20th century.

ABSTRACT EXPRESSIONISM. Art that expresses the subconscious of the artist/creator. A popular movement in the mid-20th century in the U.S. and Europe.

AMERICAN CHIPPENDALE. Furniture made in the American colonies in the mid- to late-18th century, influenced by Thomas Chippendale's well-known design books.

AMERICAN EMPIRE. The architectural furniture style from roughly 1820 to 1840, strongly influenced by France; some of Duncan Phyfe's designs are associated with the period.

ANTIQUE. Art or furniture dating from before 1840, according to U.S. Department of Customs. The term is loosely used to date furniture more than 100 years old.

ARMOIRE. French term for a movable cupboard or wardrobe; originally such cabinets were used to store armor.

ART MODERNE. Modern style of the 1920s; closely associated with French furniture and objets d'art; also called Art Deco.

ART NOUVEAU. A briefly popular art style of the late 19th and early 20th centuries based on fanciful interpretations of plants and nature that also was influenced by Japanese art and the Gothic styles of the Middle Ages; a French term for new art.

AUBUSSON. A rug woven like a tapestry; commonly refers to rugs with floral motifs made in France in the 18th and 19th centuries.

BALL-AND-CLAW FOOT. A furniture foot carved to resemble a bird's or dragon's claw holding a ball or jewel; sometimes ascribed to an ancient Chinese motif for power.

BANQUETTE. French for upholstered bench.

BARBIZON SCHOOL. Mid-19th-century landscape paintings that depicted a romantic vision of peasant life; associated with the work of Jean Francois-Millet.

BARCELONA CHAIR. Iconic 20th-century chair design by influential architect Ludwig Mies van der Rohe. The curved front legs are integral to the back while the rear legs support the seat; typically fabricated in tufted black leather.

BAUHAUS. Austrian art, architecture, and design school (1919 to 1933) that influenced 20th-century modernist movements.

BERGERE. French for upholstered armchair with enclosed sides and exposed frame; bottom cushion may be unattached.

BIEDERMEIER. The German interpretation of the 19th-century neoclassic style; the name comes from "Papa Biedermeier," a German symbol of middle-class comforts and affluence. Furniture in this style was also made in Austria and Northern Italy.

BOMBÉ. French for convex or bulging; refers to the flowing, somewhat swollen appearance of chests and commodes of the Louis XV period.

BOW FRONT. The convex front of casegoods that swells horizontally, such as chests or sideboards; the term is often associated with the English Adam and Hepplewhite styles.

BUFFET. A side or serving table with cupboards or shelves; a sideboard.

BULL'S-EYE MIRROR. Refers to a round mirror with convex or concave glass in a decorative frame; often associated with the American Federal period.

BUN FOOT. A furniture leg support that appears as a slightly flattened ball.

CABRIOLE LEG. Furniture leg that curves outward, then down; popular in 18th-century Europe and America.

CAMELBACK SOFA. Back features a serpentine line that extends from rollover arms to tallest height on the middle of the sofa back; associated with late 18th and early 19th centuries in England and America.

CANAPÉ. French for a small two-seater sofa.

CANDELABRA. Plural of candelabrum.

CANDELABRUM. A branched, ornamental candlestick; a rarely used term.

CARTOON. Italian for a full-size drawing on paper worked out as pattern for a fresco or other work of art; now collected.

CELLARETTE. A portable cabinet or liquor chest.

CHAISE LONGUE. French for long, upholstered chair with elongated seat supported by an extra pair of legs.

CHINOISERIE. Western interpretation of Asian motifs.

CHIPPENDALE. Refers to three generations of English cabinetmakers. Most influential was Thomas Chippendale II (1718–1779), whose books inspired furnituremakers on both sides of the Atlantic Ocean.

CIRCA. The year or era, used to denote date of creation.

COMMODE. French for low chest of drawers or cabinet.

CONSOLE TABLE. Table with shelf that may be designed to attach to the wall; often used in entries or foyers.

COROMANDEL SCREEN. Chinese lacquered screen.

CREDENZA. Italian for serving table or sideboard.

DEMILUNE. A semicircular piece of furniture, such as a commode or small table.

DIPTYCH. Small hinged screen with two panels; two related paintings.

EAMES CHAIR. Iconic 20th-century chair design by Charles Eames, separated chairback and seat are supported by frame.

EMPIRE. The classic revival movement (rediscovery of Ancient Greek, Roman, and Egyptian motifs) that roughly corresponded with the Napoleonic period (1804–1820) in France; popular in antebellum United States.

ENGRAVING. A method of printmaking; techniques including woodcut, etching, and mezzotint.

EPERGNE. French for an ornamental stand supporting a dish; often fabricated in glass.

ÉTAGÈRE. Hanging or freestanding open decorative shelving units for small objets d'art.

FAKE. A counterfeit copy meant to deceive.

FAUTEUIL. French for an upholstered armchair with open sides; arms are usually upholstered or feature elbow pads.

FAUVE. Early-20th-century art movement noted for bright

colors and two-dimensional images; influenced by Japanese art.

FRENCH DIRECTOIRE. A transitional period in French decorative arts (1789–1804) between Louis XVI and Empire styles; noteworthy for Revolutionary motifs.

FRENCH RÉGENCE. Transitional period (1700–1730) between Louis XIV and lighter Louis XV designs.

GEORGIAN. An epoch of fine English design during the reigns of George I, George II, and George III (1714–1811). Furniture of the periods included the original works of the Adam brothers, Chippendale, Hepplewhite, and Sheraton.

GILDED. Ornamented with gold leaf or gold dust.

GIRANDOLE. Oval or round mirror with attached candle sconces, derived from French for "branched candlestick."

GRISAILLE. A monochromatic painting in shades of gray; sometimes the base design for an oil painting.

HALL CHAIR. Sculptural decorative chairs made for halls by English and American furnituremakers.

HEPPLEWHITE, GEORGE. 18th-century English furniture designer; associated with the shieldback chair and carved motifs such as Prince of Wales feathers.

HIGHBOY. A tall chest on legs, traced to Holland and popular in Colonial America; also term for chest of drawers.

HITCHCOCK CHAIR. Chair style created by 19th-century American furnituremaker Lambert Hitchcock; frequently painted black and detailed with stenciled motifs.

HUDSON RIVER SCHOOL. 19th century American landscape paintings in the romantic style; Thomas Cole and Frederick Church are well-known artists of the school.

HUNTBOARD. Popular term for "slab," tall serving piece made in the American South in 19th century.

IMPRESSIONISM. European and later American modern art movement emphasizing light on the natural landscape; associated with 19th century French painters, including Monet, Manet, and Renoir.

JAPANNING. 18th-century enameling process to imitate the effect of Japanese lacquering.

JARDINIÈRE. French for plant container or stand.

KLISMOS. Greek chair form with concave curved back rail and saber legs, popular in form in neoclassic era.

LE CORBUSIER. Swiss architect; influenced early-20th-century modernist movement.

LITHOGRAPH. A drawing with grease pencil or crayon that can be reproduced in a limited number of printed impressions.

LOLLING CHAIR. Upholstered armchairs with exposed arms and high back, also called Martha Washington chair.

LOUIS XIV. The Baroque style was refined with neoclassic motifs during the period (1643–1715); pieces are large and grand. Foot styles included cloven-hoof and bun.

LOUIS XV. The style is considered feminine with the s-curved cabriole leg and gilt-bronze ornament (1715–1774). New domestic pieces including commodes and settees appeared under the influence of Mme. de Pompadour.

LOUIS XVI. The final Louis style rejected curves in favor of straight lines and classic motifs (1774–1793). Furniture was lighter and simpler than in the preceding Louis styles and governed by neoclassic restraint.

LOUIS-PHILIPPE PERIOD. Refers to the period that corresponds to the reign of Louis-Philippe (1830–1848); furniture is in the neoclassic direction of Louis XVI.

LOWBOY. A low chest of drawers or serving table.

MAJOLICA. Brightly colored Italian and Spanish pottery, with natural motifs such as leaves; initially popular in 19th-century England and the United States.

MORTISE-AND-TENON JOINT. Method of furniture joinery where the tenon fits snugly into the open mortise.

MURANO GLASS. Colored glass associated with Venice and the nearby island of Murano.

NEOCLASSICISM. A movement in architecture, art, and decorative arts fueled by the discoveries of the lost ancient Roman cities of Pompeii and Herculaneum.

OBJET D'ART. French for small decorative object.

ORMOLU. Gilded bronze used on furniture mounts.

PAD FOOT. Flattened, disklike foot used with a cabriole leg.

PARSONS TABLE. Plain, square table with square legs integral to the apron and table top, associated with Parsons School of Design of New York.

PAW-AND-BALL FOOT. Carved representation of a lion's or bear's paw, grasping a ball.

PEMBROKE TABLE. Originally designed in 18th-century England with a drawer set into an apron; popular in the American Federal period.

PERIOD FURNITURE. Refers to furniture newly made in a style of a previous period.

PHYFE, DUNCAN. Scottish cabinetmaker (1768–1854) who worked in the United States in Regency styles.

PIER TABLE. Console table designed to be used with pier glass or mirror.

POP ART. Art movement based on popular, primarily American culture of the 1960s; identified with entertainment and advertising.

QUEEN ANNE PERIOD. Furniture and decorative arts in England during the reign of Queen Anne (1702–1714); detailed with the cabriole leg and shell carving.

RÉCAMIER. 19th century chaise longue in the Directoire or Empire style named for Madame Récamier; has a single armrest.

REFECTORY TABLE. Long, narrow table.

REGENCY. Refers to the period in England when the future George IV was Regent (1811–1820); a neoclassic style closely related to French Directoire and Empire.

SAARINEN, EERO. Finnish-born American architect known for contemporary furniture icons including the molded pedestal chair and table.

SABER LEGS. Splayed legs seen on 19th-century chairs, tapered to resemble a cavalry saber.

SCROLL FOOT. Flattened scroll at the end of a cabriole leg.

SETTEE. Small sofa, derivative of settle.

SETTLE. Bench for two or more people with high back and high arms; traced to 17th century.

SHAGREEN. Dyed shark, horse, or mule skins used to cover furniture and decorative objects.

SHAKER. Refers to the simple, plain furniture made by an American religious sect in the 19th century.

SHIELDBACK CHAIR. Popularized by Hepplewhite, the open chair back is in the shape of a shield.

SIDEBOARD. A serving and storage piece for the dining room, perfected by Hepplewhite and Sheraton designs in late 18th century England and Colonial America.

SLEIGH BED. Notable for curved head and footboards of the same height; originally a French Empire form.

SLIPPER CHAIR. Upholstered high-back chair with a low seat and no arms.

SPADE FOOT. Tapered, rectangular foot separated from leg by raised detailing; seen in Hepplewhite designs.

SPIRAL LEG. Leg carved to resemble twisted rope. Originally Portuguese but also seen on English Sheraton pieces during the Restoration.

SPLAT. The central, upright panel of a chair back.

SPLAY LEG. A leg that angles or flares outward from a chair.

SUFFAH. An Arab word referring to reclining; believed to be the basis for "sofa."

SURREALISM. 20th-century art movement traced in part to the fantastic works of Dutch painter Hieronymus Bosch. Salvador Dalí and Pablo Picasso are associated with the movement.

TEA TABLE. English-style table introduced to Colonial America for tea drinking.

TESTER BED. Bed with four high posters of the same height and a frame for a canopy.

TOLE. French term for sheet iron; usually painted and used for lamps, shades, and decorative objects.

TORCHÉRE. In current usage, a floorlamp with the fixture mounted to cast light toward the ceiling.

TRUMEAU MIRROR. A framed mirror with a painted decorative scene, often pastoral or a carved relief above the glass; dates to the late 18th century.

TUB CHAIR. Late-18th-century English style with rounded back and low arms; typically a Sheraton-style piece.

VENETIAN. Relating to the art, decorative arts, and furniture of Venice; highly collected today, the furniture was finished with a variety of decorative techniques such as japanning (see page 189); exaggerated forms include the bombé front.

WASSILY CHAIR. Famous modern chair form designed by Marcel Breuer in 1925 and named for artist Wassily Kandinsky. Tubular steel frame with leather sling-construction.

WINDSOR CHAIR. Spindle-back wooden chair originally designed in England, popular in America from colonial times; styles are differentiated by the chair back, such as fan or hoop.

LIGHTING. Galleries, museums, architects, and interior designers are sources for referral to highly qualified lighting consultants who deal with fine art and artifacts. Architects and interior designers may also provide lighting plans.

Collectors who prefer to design their own lighting plans can work with some simple guidelines for pleasing results. The key is to build a room's overall lighting around the visual focus, using layers of ambient, accent, and wall lighting. At the most basic level, overhead and wall-mounted lighting, such as dining room chandeliers and sconces wired with dimmers, soften and help to create mood for overall ambient lighting. Depending on the size of the chandelier and the height of the ceiling, the standard distance between the bottom of the chandelier and the tabletop is 30 to 36 inches.

In addition to chandeliers or pendent lighting, recessed and track-mounted features are typical choices for room lighting that also focuses on architectural features or art. While recessed ceiling fixtures are the least obtrusive, updated mounted lighting, such as halogen spotlights on rods, works well when contemporary paintings are part of the interior design.

If a brick or stone chimney breast is the focal point, a standard way to light the art is to center two recessed accent lights in the ceiling about 12 inches from the painting. The lights are aimed so beams of light illuminate the painting and the fireplace. Frequently used specifications are for small fixtures with 50-watt MR 16 or PAR 20 bulbs in a baffled, reflector, or pinhole downlight, such as the eyeball style that extends below the ceiling, or in a compact, low-profile track fixture.

When the fireplace without the exposed chimney is set into the wall, accent lights may be mounted 18 to 30 inches from the wall for soft illumination. Wide-beam bulbs are used to light paintings; narrow beams are recommended for small objects. If several paintings are hung on a long wall, a relatively even wash of lighting is used. Recessed wall-washers may be installed in the ceiling equal distance apart and about 18 to 30 inches from the wall.

The typical wattage is 75- or 100-watt bulbs, although lower-wattage bulbs may work for a soft, serene ambience. Spacing depends on the desired effect; close spacing softens the shadows at the top of the wall. Recessed wall-washers are installed to provide dramatic, direct light to individual paintings. For a spotlit effect, the accent lights should be mounted at a 30-degree angle and the beam focused on the art. Three times the room's normal light level is required to create a focal point. Brass picture lights serve the same purpose as they attach to the frame and direct light onto the art.

If track lighting is used, small track fixtures with wide-beam bulbs are often used; fixtures are typically spaced about 24 inches apart. Smoothing lenses, available for many track fixtures, make the lighting more even.

INDEX

SPECIAL THANKS

John Barman
Jim Barrow
Jock and Day Cowperthwaite
William Diamond and Anthony Baratta
Meredith and John Dunnan
Mr. and Mrs. Frank E. Fowler
Gunkelmans Interior Design
Thad Hayes
Bill Harrison and Deborah Hodge
Jim and Phoebe Howard
Gary McBournie
Mr. and Mrs. Gill Peabody
Scott Salvator and Michael Zabriskie
Jan Showers
Laura Stoll
Robert Stilin and Waldo Fernandez
Roxanne Vogel